BARRON'S

NEW YORK STATE

GRADE 7 ENGLISH LANGUAGE ARTS TEST

Cynthia Lassonde, Ph.D.
SUNY College at Oneonta
Oneonta, NY

Melissa Wadsworth-Miller, M.A.
Tonawanda Middle School
Tonawanda, NY

DEDICATION

To the students using this book. May reading and writing be your lifelong friends. —CL

To my husband, Andrew, and my daughters, Maddie and Abbie.
Your love and support mean everything to me. —MWM

About the Authors

Cynthia A. Lassonde is an associate professor of undergraduate and graduate literacy courses at the State University of New York College at Oneonta. Previously, she taught elementary English Language Arts for more than twenty years in upstate New York. She has had leadership roles with the International Reading Association, the New York State English Council, and the New York Association of Colleges for Teacher Education. She is editor of *Excelsior: Leadership in Teaching and Learning,* author of Barron's *New York State Grade 6 English Language Arts Test,* and the 2009–2010 recipient of the SUNY Chancellor's Award for Excellence in Teaching.

Melissa Wadsworth-Miller has been teaching English for the past sixteen years at Tonawanda Middle School in the city of Tonawanda, New York. She received the New York State English Council 2005 Educator of Excellence Award, as well as the Western New York Educational Service Council's Award for Excellence in Education. In 2007 she received the New York State English Council's Program of Excellence Award. She also has authored several articles that have been published in *The English Record,* and she is the membership chairperson for the New York State English Council.

Photo credits: All photos, except as indicated, have been supplied by Shutterstock.

© Copyright 2011 by Barron's Educational Series, Inc.

All inquiries should be addressed to:
Barron's Educational Series, Inc.
250 Wireless Boulevard
Hauppauge, New York 11788
www.barronseduc.com

Library of Congress Control Number: 2010016895
ISBN: 978-0-7641-4513-1

Library of Congress Cataloging-in-Publication Data

Lassonde, Cynthia A.
   New York State grade 7 intermediate-level English language arts test / Cynthia A. Lassonde and Melissa Wadsworth-Miller.
      p. cm.
   At head of title: Barron's
   Includes index.
   ISBN-13: 978-0-7641-4513-1
   ISBN-10: 0-7641-4513-4
   1. Language arts (Middle school)—New York (State)—Examinations, questions, etc.—Study guides. 2. Middle schools—New York (State)—Examinations—Language arts.
I. Wadsworth-Miller, Melissa.   II. Title.
   LB1631.5.L38 2010
   373.126'2—dc22

2010016895

Date of Manufacture: September 2016
Manufactured by: B11R11, Robbinsville, NJ

PRINTED IN THE UNITED STATES OF AMERICA
9 8 7 6

CONTENTS

INTRODUCTION

THE NEW YORK STATE ENGLISH LANGUAGE ARTS LEARNING STANDARDS

As you probably know, your teachers plan short- and long-term goals for you. They plan lessons based on a set of skills and knowledge called the New York State Learning Standards. These Standards were published originally by the New York State Department of Education in the mid-1990s. The Standards outline the skills and knowledge all students in prekindergarten through Grade 12 must attain before graduation. They are a result of the nation's concern that all children reach certain expectations. There are Standards in

- English language arts;
- mathematics, science, and technology;
- social studies;
- the arts, and other areas.

These Standards are the core of what all students should know and be able to do by the time they leave high school.

There are four English Language Arts Learning Standards:

1. Students will read, write, listen, and speak for information and understanding.
2. Students will read, write, listen, and speak for literary response and expression.
3. Students will read, write, listen, and speak for critical analysis and evaluation.
4. Students will read, write, listen, and speak for social interaction.

Figure 1 shows some examples of what the four Learning Standards include in the seventh grade.

Standard 1: Language for Information and Understanding

Can you

■ synthesize information from a variety of resources to produce oral and written reports,

■ take an authoritative stance on an issue and back your position with valid references, and

■ connect new information to your prior knowledge and experiences?

Standard 2: Language for Literary Response and Expression

Can you

■ identify the characteristics of different types of texts and literary elements,

■ recognize multiple levels of meaning within a text, and

■ write interpretive essays that comment on the significance of texts?

Standard 3: Language for Critical Analysis and Evaluation

Can you

■ develop arguments based on evidence that effectively influence your readers,

■ evaluate the accuracy and validity of information, and

■ recognize how one's point of view can influence his or her perspective?

Standard 4: Language for Social Interaction

Can you

■ recognize the type of language that is appropriate in various situations,

■ respectfully express your ideas and concerns in discussions, and

■ consider how the way you communicate will be received by others?

Figure 1 Examples of Grade 7 English Language Arts Learning Standards

THE MISSION OF THE TESTING PROGRAM

To determine whether or not students were attaining mastery of the state Standards, New York State developed a set of examinations to be administered annually. The exams assess Standards 1, 2, and 3. To meet the No Child Left Behind requirements, state English language arts tests are now given annually in Grade 3 through Grade 8. The tests aim to measure student progress to ensure you are meeting grade-level criteria. They are not used, however, as the only measurement for students to move on to the next grade. You are not retained in a grade just because you do poorly on these state tests. The tests are used as indicators, though, to see if you need extra help. They are also helpful in acquiring extra training and assistance for teachers and school districts.

HOW TO USE THIS BOOK

This book is written for seventh graders to use not only as a test preparation guide but also as a handbook to learn and practice effective reading, writing, listening, and test-taking strategies. You can use this book by yourself or along with your class as a classroom textbook. The information and practice tests provided within the pages of this guide will help you develop valuable and efficient strategies that will help you with most subjects through your high school years. When you become proficient with the strategies in this book, you will be a confident test taker who is equipped with the literacy skills required to do well on the Grade 7 English language arts test.

This handbook begins with a diagnostic test, complete with explained answers. You should start by completing the diagnostic test to become familiar with the test format and to determine which parts of the test may be more problematic for you than others. Then, as you work your way through the book, focus intently on the parts of the diagnostic test that caused problems for you.

Chapter 1 provides an overview of the test. You will learn what the test is composed of, your responsibilities, and how your responses will be scored. By learning about the test, you will be able to predict what the test will be like. Knowing what to expect on a test can put you at ease so you can better focus on the job that lies ahead. Also, you'll have an informed idea of how to prepare for the test.

Chapters 2 and 3 are the strategy chapters. Strategies are like tools in a toolbox. When you run into a problem, you reach into the toolbox and pull out the appropriate, useful tool for the job. The tool helps you unlock the passage just like a screwdriver would loosen a tightly turned screw. Strategies help you solve problems.

By presenting scientifically based, research-proven strategies that have been shown to be beneficial in promoting your literacy skills, these chapters provide a firm foundation for you as you learn to apply the strategies in the following chapters and to the Grade 7 ELA test. Chapter 2 is divided into reading strategies, writing strategies, editing strategies, and listening and note-taking strategies. Chapter 3 focuses on test-taking strategies. Throughout the book, you are encouraged to think about which strategies you are using until you begin to use them automatically. You should use Chapters 2 and 3 as resources. Read through them, but then continually revisit them to select the necessary tools for a particular problem.

Chapters 4, 5, and 6 look separately at each of the three books that make up the Grade 7 test. These chapters are formatted in a similar sequence so you become familiar and comfortable with their contents and flow. Basically, you will learn about the contents of each book, you will practice appropriate strategies that will help you with the tasks in that book, and you will complete sample test questions. The answers are given and explained in Appendix C. A think-aloud approach talks you through the thought process used to successfully answer the questions. Possible helpful strategies are explained.

Two complete practice tests can be found at the end of the book. Answers and explanations follow each test. As you work through these practice tests, replicate as closely as possible the test conditions you will encounter on test days. Prepare exactly as you plan to, find someone to read the listening section to you, and ask someone to time each part of the test for you.

The appendix includes descriptions of literary genres; a glossary of terms you should know; and the answers to the sample questions in Chapters 4, 5, and 6. Throughout the book, important terms are highlighted in blue the first time they are used. These terms are explained more fully in the glossary (Appendix B).

A PERSONAL FINAL WORD

Do you want to improve your reading, writing, listening, and test-taking skills? Do you want to do well on the state tests? Then you are on your way. Being motivated and eager to do your best are probably the most important factors in improving your skills and in doing well on tests. By studying and putting effort into doing the practice exercises in this book, you are taking advantage of this opportunity to improve your literacy skills and to learn and practice new strategies. These strategies and practice will help you do your best on the Grade 7 ELA test. Good luck!

DIAGNOSTIC TEST

This diagnostic test is a condensed version of the actual test. All parts of the test are included; however, the actual test will have more passages and more multiple-choice questions in Book 1: Reading.

HOW TO USE YOUR RESULTS

The purpose of this diagnostic test is to give you an idea of what the test will be like and to help you determine which parts of the test might be more problematic for you than others. For example, if you miss several questions in the reading section of the test, study those strategies in Chapter 2 and work diligently through Chapter 4. If you have trouble with the listening passage, be sure to study carefully the listening strategies and description of that part of the test as presented in Chapters 2 and 5. If you want to improve your skills for the reading and writing part of the test, study the reading, writing, and editing strategies in Chapter 2 and read carefully while working through Chapter 6 and the practice tests.

TEST

BOOK 1: READING

In Book 1, you will read some passages and answer several questions about each one. You may make notes or marks on the test pages as you read. Fill in the answers to the multiple-choice questions on the tear-out bubble sheet on the next page. Be sure to answer all of the questions. The correct answers, with explanations, can be found at the end of this test, on page 37.

ANSWER SHEET

BOOK 1

1. Ⓐ Ⓑ Ⓒ Ⓓ   5. Ⓐ Ⓑ Ⓒ Ⓓ   9. Ⓐ Ⓑ Ⓒ Ⓓ

2. Ⓐ Ⓑ Ⓒ Ⓓ   6. Ⓐ Ⓑ Ⓒ Ⓓ   10. Ⓐ Ⓑ Ⓒ Ⓓ

3. Ⓐ Ⓑ Ⓒ Ⓓ   7. Ⓐ Ⓑ Ⓒ Ⓓ

4. Ⓐ Ⓑ Ⓒ Ⓓ   8. Ⓐ Ⓑ Ⓒ Ⓓ

BOOK 2

1. Ⓐ Ⓑ Ⓒ Ⓓ   5. Ⓐ Ⓑ Ⓒ Ⓓ

2. Ⓐ Ⓑ Ⓒ Ⓓ   6. Ⓐ Ⓑ Ⓒ Ⓓ

3. Ⓐ Ⓑ Ⓒ Ⓓ   7. Ⓐ Ⓑ Ⓒ Ⓓ

4. Ⓐ Ⓑ Ⓒ Ⓓ   8. Ⓐ Ⓑ Ⓒ Ⓓ

For questions 9–11, write your responses on the test pages.

BOOK 3

Write your responses on the test pages.

BOOK 1: READING

Directions: Read the following essay. Then answer questions 1 through 4.

THE CONTRIBUTIONS OF ANCIENT GREECE

Akshar Shastri

The ancient Greeks helped civilizations all over the world with their contributions in literature, art, and science. Modern-day Western civilization is one of the many civilizations that the Greeks helped through their pursuit of perfection and their search for knowledge. The influence of the Greeks on Western civilization can be seen very clearly in architecture, government, and mathematics.

Architecture is an extremely important asset to any culture, and one can see influences of Greek architecture in America. Some of the most iconic buildings of American culture, such as the White House and the Supreme Court, use columns, stairs, and other design aspects that are similar to those seen on the Parthenon. Although the classical architecture displayed in ancient Greece is relatively simple, the fact that it is used today in some of America's most prestigious

Ruins of the Parthenon

buildings shows that Greek architecture carries a status with it in the American society.

The United States uses a system of government called a democratic republic. The ancient Greeks were the first people to come up with a democracy. Pericles stated that he wanted a government that favored the many over the few. He wanted all citizens to have equal opportunities to serve the public, much like our system today. American democracy is based on the people holding the power, just like ancient Greece.

Finally, contributions to the field of mathematics have probably been most universally accepted. Euclid was a Greek mathematician who excelled in geometry and developed many theorems used in math today. For example, he came up with the theorem that vertical angles are congruent. This observation, along with many others, influenced Western civilization, as well as Eastern civilizations.

The Greek civilization had a global impact across the world. Many ideas and customs that people follow today are based on principles founded by the ancient Greeks. The United States and many other nations will always remain indebted to the contributions made by the Greek civilization.

1. How does the author support the idea that the ancient Greeks influenced the architecture of America?

   A. by comparing the materials used in Greek and American structures

   B. by implying that all of our government buildings were built by Greeks

   C. by pointing out similar features, such as the use of columns and stairs

   D. by describing how the governments are similar

2. Which statement **best** supports the idea that Pericles was Greek and not American?

   A. The ancient Greeks were the first people to come up with a democracy.

   B. Pericles stated that he wanted a government that favored the many over the few.

   C. He wanted all citizens to have equal opportunities to serve the public, much like our system today.

   D. American democracy is based on the people holding the power, just like ancient Greece.

3. Read this sentence from the passage:

Finally, contributions to the field of mathematics have probably been most universally accepted.

In this sentence, the phrase "universally accepted" means

   A. used and acknowledged by mathematicians around the world

   B. mathematics is used to calculate universal distances

   C. the Greeks were the wisest mathematicians in history

   D. mathematics strengthen our democracy

4. Which statement **best** summarizes this passage?

   A. Ancient civilizations contributed a great deal to the Western civilization.

   B. Ancient Greeks contributed a lot to our society.

   C. The ancient Greek civilization influenced the architecture, government, and mathematics of the Western world.

   D. The architecture, government, and mathematics of the ancient Greeks were superior to those of any other civilizations of the time.

Directions: Read this excerpt from "The Bells" by Edgar Allan Poe. Then answer questions 5 through 7.

Runic—an ancient Germanic language

Tintinnabulation—the ringing of bells

EXCERPT FROM "THE BELLS"

Edgar Allan Poe

I

Hear the sledges with the bells—
Silver bells!
What a world of merriment their melody foretells!
How they tinkle, tinkle, tinkle,
In the icy air of night!
While the stars that oversprinkle
All the heavens seem to twinkle
With a crystalline delight;
Keeping time, time, time,
In a sort of Runic rhyme,
To the tintinnabulation that so musically wells
From the bells, bells, bells, bells,
Bells, bells, bells—
From the jingling and the tinkling of the bells.

II

Hear the mellow wedding bells—
Golden bells!
What a world of happiness their harmony foretells!
Through the balmy air of night
How they ring out their delight!
From the molten-golden notes,
And all in tune,
What a liquid ditty floats
To the turtle-dove that listens, while she gloats

On the moon!
Oh, from out the sounding cells
What a gush of euphony voluminously wells!
How it swells!
How it dwells
On the Future!—how it tells
Of the rapture that impels
To the swinging and the ringing
Of the bells, bells, bells,
Of the bells, bells, bells, bells,
Bells, bells, bells—
To the rhyming and the chiming of the bells!

5. Read the following lines from the poem:

   From the bells, bells, bells, bells,
   Bells, bells, bells—
   From the jingling and the tinkling of the bells.

   This is an example of

   A. meter

   B. metaphor

   C. personification

   D. simile

6. Read the following lines from the poem:

   To the turtle-dove that listens, while she gloats
   On the moon!

   This is an example of

   A. contrast

   B. onomatopoeia

   C. personification

   D. simile

7. Read the following lines from the poem:

Hear the sledges with the bells—
Silver bells!
What a world of merriment their melody foretells!
How they tinkle, tinkle, tinkle,
In the icy air of night!

With these lines, the poet **most likely** creates which of the following images for the reader?

A. a hammer with bells on it

B. an elf with bells on his shirt dancing through the forest on a snowy night

C. a sleigh full of laughing people going down the lane on a cold evening

D. a group of people singing and ringing bells on a cold night

Directions: Read the following essay. Then answer questions 8 and 9.

THE DOG AND THE WOLF

A gaunt wolf was almost dead with hunger when he happened to meet a house-dog who was passing by.

"Ah, Cousin," said the dog. "I knew how it would be; your irregular life will soon be the ruin of you. Why do you not work steadily as I do, and get your food regularly given to you?"

"I would have no objection," said the wolf, "if I could only get a place."

"I will easily arrange that for you," said the dog. "Come with me to my master, and you shall share my work."

So, the wolf and the dog went toward the town together. On the way there, the wolf noticed that the hair on a certain part of the dog's neck was very much worn away, so he asked him how that had come about.

"Oh, it is nothing," said the dog. "That is only the place where the collar is put on at night to keep me chained up. It chafes a bit, but one soon gets used to it."

"Is that all?" said the wolf. "Then goodbye to you, Master Dog."

8. What is **most likely** the moral of this fable?

   A. One good turn deserves another.

   B. It is best to prepare for the days ahead.

   C. Gratitude is the sign of noble souls.

   D. It is better to starve free than to be a fat slave.

9. **Most likely**, the wolf was going to go with the dog at first because

   A. he wanted a friend

   B. he had no objection and had nothing else to do

   C. he was hungry

   D. he was injured and needed help

Directions: Read this poem. Then answer question 10.

THE STRINGY-BARK TREE

Henry Lawson

There's the whitebox and pine on the ridges afar,
Where the iron-bark, blue-gum, and peppermint are;
There is many another, but dearest to me,
And the king of them all was the stringy-bark tree.

Then of stringy-bark slabs were the walls of the hut,
And from stringy-bark saplings the rafters were cut;
And the roof that long sheltered my brothers and me
Was of broad sheets of bark from the stringy-bark tree.

And when sawn-timber homes were built out in the West,
Then for walls and for ceilings its wood was the best;
And for shingles and palings to last while men be,
There was nothing on earth like the stringy-bark tree.

Far up the long gullies the timber-trucks went,
Over tracks that seemed hopeless, by bark hut and tent;
And the gaunt timber-finder, who rode at his ease,
Led them on to a gully of stringy-bark trees.

Now still from the ridges, by ways that are dark,
Come the shingles and palings they call stringy-bark;
Though you ride through long gullies a twelve months you'll see
But the old whitened stumps of the stringy-bark tree.

10. What is **most likely** the message the poet is trying to convey to readers through this poem?

   A. Human development can have detrimental effects on our natural resources.

   B. Stringy-bark trees are very useful for a variety of purposes.

   C. The author's life wouldn't have been the same without the stringy-bark trees.

   D. People will never again be able to harvest stringy-bark trees for houses.

BOOK 2: LISTENING AND WRITING MECHANICS

For this part of the test, carefully cut out the following passage, and find someone to read the directions and definitions below and the passage on the following page to you. The reader should carefully and clearly read the passage to you two times as you take notes. Answers and explanations appear at the end of the test, on pages 38–40.

Directions: **You will hear a passage called "Lacrosse, Yesterday and Today" by Melissa Wadsworth-Miller. You will listen to the passage two times. You may take notes at any time as you listen to the passage. Then you will use your notes to help you answer the questions that follow. Your answers to these questions will show your understanding of the passage.**

Here are some words you will need to know as you listen to the passage:

▪ ritual—ceremony

▪ missionary—somebody doing church work abroad

LACROSSE, YESTERDAY AND TODAY

Melissa Wadsworth-Miller

Lacrosse is a game that is quickly gaining a reputation at high schools and colleges across the United States. The formation of the Major League Lacrosse organization has also made the sport more popular. But how much does the average person know about the origins and rules of this game?

Lacrosse is a game that requires a marked field with goals on either end; a small, solid rubber ball; and lacrosse sticks for each of the players. A lacrosse stick looks like a long-handled racquet. On the head of the stick is loose netting that is made to hold the lacrosse ball when it is thrown or caught. The object of the game is to use the lacrosse stick to catch, carry, and pass the ball in order to score points by throwing the ball into the opponent's net. Meanwhile, members of the opposite team try to capture the ball with blocks and body checks so they can score against their opponent.

Did you know that, although lacrosse is a French name, this game originated with the Native Americans of North America? The Iroquois were one of the first Native American tribes to play lacrosse. The sport was often played as part of religious rituals. However, it was also used to resolve conflicts, heal the sick, and prepare young men for war. Early lacrosse required deep spiritual involvement. Players took on the roles of warriors with the goal of bringing honor to themselves, their tribes, and their Creator. It was often referred to as "the Creator's game." Legend states that sometimes games consisted of more than 100 players from different tribes. Lacrosse fields could be many miles long and wide, and the games could last for days.

Jean de Brébeuf, a French Jesuit missionary, was the first European to write about the game. In 1637 he saw Iroquois tribesmen playing it, and legend says he called it *le jeu de la crosse* after the French term for field hockey. However, European immigrants to North America did not begin playing lacrosse until 1856. This is when Dr. William George Beers, a Canadian dentist, founded the Montreal Lacrosse Club. Beers created a proper set of rules for the game, shortened the length of each match, and limited the number of players to twelve per team. By the early 1900s, colleges, universities, and high schools across Canada were playing the sport; however, it had not yet received national exposure in the United States. It was primarily a regional sport that centered in Maryland, upstate New York, and the New England states.

Love of the sport has spread quickly in the twenty-first century. States in the southern United States, such as Georgia, Alabama, and Florida, have adopted lacrosse; states in the West and Midwest are following their lead. Lacrosse crossed gender barriers with the formation of the National Collegiate Athletic Association Women's Lacrosse Division I in 1982, and there are currently 14 countries that have national lacrosse leagues. Many fans would like to see lacrosse become an Olympic sport. If lacrosse continues to spread like it has over the past century, a future Olympic lacrosse match may not be too far off.

NOTES

NOTES

Multiple-Choice Questions

1. According to the passage, what ethnic group created lacrosse?

   A. Canadians

   B. Native Americans

   C. The French

   D. Americans

2. In the beginning, lacrosse was played for all of the following reasons **except**

   A. to heal the sick

   B. as part of a religious ritual

   C. to resolve conflicts

   D. to win territory

3. Read the following sentences:

   It had not yet received national exposure in the United States. It was primarily a regional sport that centered in Maryland, upstate New York, and the New England states.

   Based on the sentences, the word *regional* means

   A. nationwide

   B. public

   C. native

   D. local

4. The information in this passage would be **most helpful** for a person who wanted to

   A. learn the rules of lacrosse

   B. learn about the person who invented the lacrosse rules

   C. understand how lacrosse changed over time

   D. join a lacrosse league

5. Which of the following sentences uses correct spelling?

   A. Players took on roles with the goal of bringing honor to there tribes and there Creator.

   B. Players took on roles with the goal of bringing honor to there tribes and they're Creator.

   C. Players took on roles with the goal of bringing honor to their tribes and there Creator.

   D. Players took on roles with the goal of bringing honor to their tribes and their Creator.

6. Read the following quote:

   Lacrosse fields could be many miles long and wide, and the games could last for days.

   The statement above is an example of a

   A. complex sentence

   B. compound sentence

   C. sentence fragment

   D. run-on sentence

7. Read the following quote:

   On the head of the stick is loose netting that is made to hold the lacrosse ball when it is caught.

   What tense are the verbs in this sentence?

   A. future tense

   B. present tense

   C. past tense

   D. perfect tense

8. Read the following sentence:

Many fans would like to see lacrosse become an olympic sport.

Which word needs to be capitalized?

A. fans

B. lacrosse

C. olympic

D. sport

Short-Response Questions

9. Complete the following chart with information from the passage.

People from Lacrosse History	Their Influence on the Game of Lacrosse
The Iroquois	
Jean de Brébeuf	
Dr. William George Beers	

10. The game of lacrosse has been around for centuries. However, today's version of the game is very different from the original. Explain how today's lacrosse is different from the form that was played in the 1600s. Use details from the passage to support your point.

_____

_____

_____

_____

_____

_____

_____

11. Read the following quote:

Love of the sport has spread quickly in the twenty-first century.

Is this statement a fact or an opinion. Use details from the passage to support your point.

_____

_____

_____

_____

_____

BOOK 3: READING AND WRITING

Directions: Book 3 asks you to write about two passages you will read. When you write your responses, be sure to

- Clearly organize your ideas

- Clearly express your ideas

- Completely and accurately answer the questions

- Support the ideas in your responses by examples from the passage or passages

- Make your writing enjoyable and interesting to the reader

One passage you will read is an excerpt from a book called *The Boys' Life of Mark Twain* by Albert Bigelow Paine. The author describes how Mark Twain, the author of *The Adventures of Tom Sawyer* and *The Adventures of Huckleberry Finn*, based his novels on his own life adventures and acquaintances. The other passage is a short story by Scott Niven called "A Torch Is Passed (Stolen)." In this story, you will meet Will, who has a strong opinion of Mark Twain. Use what you learn from the passages to answer questions 1 through 5.

Sample responses are at the end of the test, on pages 41–43.

Mark Twain was the pen-name the author Samuel Clemens wrote under and signed to his many, many books, such as *The Adventures of Tom Sawyer* and *The Adventures of Huckleberry Finn*.

EXCERPT FROM *THE BOYS' LIFE OF MARK TWAIN*

Albert Bigelow Paine

In beginning *The Adventures of Tom Sawyer* the author says, "Most of the adventures recorded in this book really occurred," and he tells us that Huck Finn is drawn from life; Tom Sawyer also, though not from a single individual, being a composite of three boys whom Mark Twain had known.

The three boys were himself, almost entirely, with traces of two schoolmates, John Briggs and Will Bowen. John Briggs was also the original of Joe Harper, the "Terror of the Seas." As for Huck Finn, the "Red-Handed," his original was a village waif named Tom Blankenship, who needed no change for his part in the story.

The Blankenship family picked up an uncertain livelihood, fishing and hunting, and lived at first under a tree in a bark shanty, but later moved into a large, barn-like building, back of the Clemens home on Hill Street. There were three male members of the household: Old Ben, the father, shiftless and dissolute; young Ben, the eldest son—a doubtful character, with certain good traits; and Tom—that is to say, Huck, who was just as he is described in the book—a ruin of rags, a river-rat, kind of heart, and accountable for his conduct to nobody in the world. He could come and go as he chose; he never had to work or go to school; he could do all the things, good and bad, that other boys longed to do and were forbidden. To them he was the symbol of liberty; his knowledge of fishing, trapping, signs, and of the woods and river gave value to his society, while the fact that it was forbidden made it necessary to Sam Clemens's happiness.

They had a wide field of action: they ranged from Holliday's Hill on the north to the cave on the south, and over the fields and through all the woods between. They explored both banks of the river, the islands, and the deep wilderness of the Illinois shore. They could run like turkeys and swim like ducks; they could handle a boat as if born in one. No orchard or melon-patch was entirely safe from them. No dog or slave patrol was so watchful that they did not sooner or later elude it. They borrowed boats with or without the owner's consent—it did not matter.

The adventures of Sam Clemens and his comrades would fill several books of the size of Tom Sawyer. Many of them are, of course, forgotten now, but those still remembered show that Mark Twain had plenty of real material.

It can be no harm now to confess that the boy Sam Clemens—a pretty small boy, a good deal less than twelve at the time, and by no means large for his years—was the leader of this unhallowed band. In any case, truth requires this admission. If the band had a leader, it was Sam, just as it was Tom Sawyer in the book. They were always ready to listen to him—they would even stop fishing to do that—and to follow his plans. They looked to him for ideas and directions, and he gloried in being a leader and showing off, just as Tom did in the book. It seems almost a pity that in those far-off barefoot days he could not have looked down the years and caught a glimpse of his splendid destiny.

But of literary fame he could never have dreamed.

Short-Response Questions

1. In the chart that follows, identify one way that we know of from this excerpt that Sam Clemens was like Tom Sawyer and one way he was not.

How Sam Was Like Tom	How Sam Was Unlike Tom

2. The author writes:

> It seems almost a pity that in those far-off barefoot days he could not have looked down the years and caught a glimpse of his splendid destiny.

Explain what the author might mean by this statement, using details from the excerpt.

_____

_____

_____

_____

_____

_____

_____

_____

The character Will in this short story is William Faulkner, who, as an adult, was a very successful Nobel Prize-winning American author.

THE TORCH IS PASSED (STOLEN)

Scott Niven

Will bought the boots on Sunday. By Wednesday, they looked worn in, used.

"Why do you wear those?" asked his mother. "They're five sizes too big."

But Will knew what he was doing. He baked the boots in the sun, fading their color from a rich brown to a dull auburn. He frayed the laces with a hunting knife. He walked through a nearby forest, careful to scuff the soles. And he stepped in puddle after puddle, letting the water seep through the shoelace holes to dampen his feet.

Five weeks later, he was ready. He crept toward the secluded lake, boots in hand, mindful of the time. It wouldn't do for him to arrive too early or too late. When the familiar clump of honeysuckle appeared on his right, he ducked behind it.

The creature of habit had arrived ahead of him. On a dead tree limb, out of reach of animals but not out of reach for an 8-year-old boy, hung the clothes and boots of the nearby swimmer. Will slid out of hiding, judged the differences between the hanging boots and his own to be unimportant, switched the boots, then took off running down the path.

His plan had worked. He had stolen the boots of one of the greatest literary geniuses of his time—Mark Twain. Now he too could create stories of Southern greatness.

Content with his crime, William Faulkner shuffled back to his house, wearing the oversized boots and dreaming of the many wonderful stories he could now write.

Short-Response Questions

3. Complete the chart to describe three of young Will's character traits. Identify details from the short story that support each trait.

Character Traits	Supporting Details from the Story

4. Why did Will take such care in scuffing the boots and fraying the laces instead of just taking Twain's boots and running away with them? Support your response with details from the story.

_____

_____

_____

_____

_____

_____

_____

_____

PLANNING PAGE

You may PLAN your writing for question 5 on this page. Write your final response on the lines on the next pages.

Extended-Response Question

5. If Mark Twain had caught Will switching boots, what do you think he would have said to him? Write your response as if you were Mark Twain talking directly to Will as he was caught red-handed making the switch. Base your answer on what you know about Twain's own boyhood adventures from *The Boys' Life of Mark Twain* and what you know about Will's purpose for stealing Twain's boots in "A Torch Is Passed (Stolen)."

In your answer, be sure to

- write as if you were Mark Twain and you had just caught Will switching the boots;

- include details from both passages to support your response as Twain;

- check your grammar, spelling, and punctuation.

_____

_____

_____

_____

_____

_____

_____

_____

_____

_____

_____

_____

_____

_____

_____

_____

_____

_____

_____

_____

_____

_____

_____

_____

_____

_____

_____

_____

_____

_____

_____

_____

_____

_____

_____

_____

ANSWERS
BOOK 1: READING

"The Contributions of Ancient Greece"

1. **C** The author does not compare materials, imply anything about government buildings, or tell how the governments are similar. The answer is literally in the passage. "Architecture" is used in the topic sentence of the paragraph that talks about columns. The question is about architecture, and choice C mentions columns and stairs.

2. **C** With the phrase "much like our system today," choice C tells the reader that Pericles lived in ancient Greece rather than in America today.

3. **A** Greek contributions to the field of mathematics were more widely accepted than their contributions to government and architecture.

4. **C** Choice C is the best summary because it includes the three specific types of contributions rather than a general discussion.

"The Bells"

5. **A** These lines repeat the word *bells* using very distinct meter. There is no use of metaphor, personification, or simile in these lines.

6. **C** The poem personifies the turtle-dove by saying that it listens and gloats, what we think of as human actions. There is no use of alliteration, onomatopoeia, or simile in these lines.

7. **C** Clues that this is a sleigh full of laughing people at night include "sledges with the bells," "world of merriment," and "icy air of night."

"The Dog and the Wolf"

8. **D** The wolf didn't want to be chained and live like a slave even if it meant he would be well fed.

9. **C** The first sentence says the wolf was "almost dead with hunger."

"The Stringy-Bark Tree"

10. **A** Although the other choices may be true, they do not have the impact on the reader that choice A would have as a message from the author.

BOOK 2: LISTENING AND WRITING MECHANICS

Multiple-Choice Questions

1. **B** All of the other groups played a role in the history of lacrosse, but Native Americans were the first ethnic group to play the game.

2. **D** All of the other reasons are discussed in the passage **except** the idea of gaining territory if a lacrosse game is won.

3. **D** There are several context clues to help the reader figure this out, such as the phrase "not yet received national exposure" and the listing of the states that play lacrosse. These clues make *local* the best synonym.

4. **C** Choices A and B are discussed in the passage, but they are not the main ideas of the article. Choice D is not covered at all, so this answer should be eliminated.

5. **D** *Their* should be spelled *their* in both cases because it is being used to show possession. *There* is used to show location, and *they're* is a contraction that actually means *they are*.

6. **B** This is an example of a compound sentence because the section *before* the comma and the section *after* the comma can stand alone as independent sentences. It is not a complex sentence because it does not contain a dependent clause. It is not a sentence fragment because it contains both a noun and a verb to make it complete. A run-on sentence is a sentence without the appropriate punctuation and/or conjunctions to join or separate the two sentences properly; this is not the case with the quoted sentence.

7. **A** The verbs *made, hold,* and *caught* are all future tense because they include the helping verb *is* before each of them. By themselves, *made* and *caught* are past tense and *hold* is present tense. In the context of the sentence, however, with the helping verb *is* they become future tense.

8. **C** *Olympic* should be capitalized because it is a proper noun. It is the name of a specific series of sporting events that occur internationally every two years.

Short-Response Questions

9.

People from Lacrosse History	Their Influence on the Game of Lacrosse
The Iroquois	The first people to play lacrosse
Jean de Brébeuf	The first European to write about the game
Dr. William George Beers	The person who created the rules for the game

10. Your answer should be similar to the paragraph below:

Today's lacrosse is very different from the form of the game that was played in the 1600s by Native Americans. One major difference is the reason for playing the game. When it was played by the Iroquois and other tribes, it was often a religious ritual or training for war. Today the game is played by college students and professional leagues for entertainment. Another difference is the number of players per team. In the past, the tribes could have hundreds of players on each team, but today's game has a limit to the number of players allowed on the field at a time.

Other possible differences include the size of the field and the length of the matches.

11. Your answer should be similar to the paragraph below:

The quote, "The love of the sport has spread very quickly during the twenty-first century" is a fact. People in several southern states, such as Georgia, Alabama, and Florida, have begun playing organized lacrosse games. States in the West and Midwest are starting to organize lacrosse teams as well. Finally, there are fourteen countries that have national lacrosse leagues. Many fans would like to see lacrosse become a sport that is played in the Olympics.

Another possible detail to include in the answer is the creation of the National Collegiate Athletic Association Women's Lacrosse Division I.

BOOK 3: READING AND WRITING

Excerpt from *The Boys' Life of Mark Twain*

Short-Response Questions

1. The graphic organizer should be completed with details directly from the passage. Here are some of the possible answers.

How Sam Was Like Tom	How Sam Was Unlike Tom
He was the leader of a band of friends who were always ready to listen to him.	Sam was a real person; Tom was a fictitious character created by Sam.

2. The short response to this question should be similar to the following:

The author might have meant by this statement that if Sam Clemens only knew how talented a writer he was and how famous he was going to become because of his writing, he might have spent his time as a young boy differently. He might have earned money writing at a younger age. He might have been more careful not to have gotten into trouble by borrowing boats without the owners' consents and by stealing fruits and melons.

"The Torch Is Passed (Stolen)"

Short-Response Questions

3. The graphic organizer should be completed with details directly from the passage. Here are some of the possible answers.

Character Traits	Supporting Details From the Story
Calculating	He arrived just in time—not too early or not too late—so Mark Twain had arrived ahead of him and was already in the water.
Deceptive	He stole Mark Twain's boots by making his own boots look like Mark's.
Hopeful	He hoped that by possessing Twain's boots, he would be able to create "stories of Southern greatness," too.

4. The short response to this question should be similar to the following:

Will looks at Mark Twain as "one of the greatest literary geniuses of his time." He respects and idolizes the author and his work. He refers to Twain's stories as "Southern greatness." Will doesn't intend to hurt or offend Twain in any way. That's why he is so sneaky and deceptive. We know he doesn't ever want Twain to find out his boots were switched because he says, "the differences between the hanging boots and his own [were] unimportant."

Extended-Response Question

5. Your answer should be similar to the response that follows. Be sure you spoke as if you were Mark Twain. You did not have to include Will's voice as was done here, though.

Twain: "What are you doing there, boy? Why, you're taking my boots, aren't you? Now, why would you be doing that?"

Will: "I don't know, sir. I guess I thought if I wore your boots I'd become a famous writer like you."

Twain: "Well, maybe you've got something there! But, you're more likely to become a writer if you write about your adventures as a boy like I did in my books The Adventures of Tom Sawyer and The Adventures of Huckleberry Finn. What I do when I write is I take little pieces of people I knew as a kid and mold them together to make a really good character that people will like to read about. Huck Finn was just like a boy I used to hang around with named Tom Blankenship; and Tom Sawyer was partly like me and partly like two schoolmates of mine—Will Bowen and John Briggs. You see, that's how you become a writer. Think about the people you know and the adventures you've had, and write about them. You could go home right now and write about this adventure about the idea you had to switch boots with me but then you got caught. What other adventures could you write about?"

OVERVIEW OF THE NEW YORK STATE GRADE 7 ENGLISH LANGUAGE ARTS TEST

This chapter gives you answers to some of the most frequently asked questions about the New York State Grade 7 Intermediate-Level English Language Arts test, from here on referred to as the New York State ELA test. The ideas explained in this chapter will clarify the purpose of the test, the parts of the test, how the test is scored, and what your responsibilities are. It will also share some online resources that will help you sharpen your literacy skills and prepare for the test.

WHAT IS THE PURPOSE OF THE TEST?

Schools in New York State require students to take a state test in English Language Arts every year from Grade 3 through Grade 8. Why do we make time in an already-full school year for these tests?

Simply put, these tests help your family, your school administrators, your teachers, and you think about how your teachers can do their best to teach you. Learning Standards indicate what a student should know and be able to do as a result of instruction. When students do well on the state ELA tests, we can assume your schooling is on track and should continue down the same successful path. However, if you do not do well on the tests or certain parts of the tests, it means we have to look more closely at what we are doing and what your specific learning needs are. Your teachers will look for teaching methods and materials that will help your peers and you to be more successful learners. Your family and you will think about what you can do to improve your learning. In short, you take these tests so we can figure out how to help you become a well-developed, literate person in today's world.

The purpose of the Grade 7 ELA test is to assess your progress in achieving the Learning Standards that have been constructed to define what all students across the state should know at this level. Your teachers, your family, and you want to be sure that daily classroom lessons and your yearly progress are both on the right path—that is, the path that allows you to reach the goals of the New York State Learning Standards. The state ELA tests are all about you and what you need to be successful. Therefore, it is for your own benefit that you do your best on these tests. This book aims to help you do that.

WHAT IS THE TEST LIKE?

If you've lived in New York State for a year or more, you surely have already taken a state ELA test. You've probably noticed, though, that each year the tests are a bit different. The tasks are different, and the readings vary. For example, the Grade 7 test is similar to the Grade 6 test in that it assesses the same Standards; however, the Grade 7 test is different in that it includes more complex passages and questions. Each year the tests reflect higher expectations for your literacy skills than the previous year. You might find the vocabulary and reading level of the Grade 7 test more difficult than you did in previous years.

If this is the first time you will be taking a New York State ELA test, the more you know about the test, the more comfortable you will feel when you actually sit down to take it. As you read this chapter, highlight the parts that you think are most important to remember. With a pencil, jot in the margins any questions that come to mind as you are reading. Ask your teacher or a family member to help you answer these questions before you take the test. Also, to learn even more about the test and the Learning Standards, look at some of the sites listed in the helpful online resources section at the end of this chapter.

The Grade 7 ELA test is given late in the spring of each year over several days. It consists of three parts; each part is called a book. Each part is timed. Figure 1.1 gives more information about the test schedule, timing, and the types of questions on the test. For a short-response question, you will write a short answer. You might complete a graphic organizer (such as a web or Venn diagram) or write a three- to five-sentence response to a question. You will also have an opportunity to show how well you can write an extended, longer response. You will demonstrate your understanding of a listening and reading selection by writing text-based responses. You will show how you would fix errors in grammar, capitalization, punctuation, or language use. For each multiple-choice question, you will select the correct response from four choices.

Book	Selection	Approximate Test Time (minutes)
1	READING 41 multiple-choice questions	70
2	LISTENING AND WRITING MECHANICS 8 multiple-choice questions 3 short-response questions	30
3	READING AND WRITING 4 short-response questions 1 extended-response question	60

Figure 1.1 Test Scheduling Information

WHAT MATERIALS DO I NEED TO BRING?

Bring two or three no. 2 pencils with erasers. Sharpen all of the pencils before the test. Try out the erasers to make sure they leave a clean page, not a smear, when you use them. Your teacher will provide all the other testing materials, such as test books and answer sheets.

WHAT ARE MY RESPONSIBILITIES?

It is your responsibility to be sure you

- are ready for the test,
- listen closely to the directions,
- read the passages carefully and closely,
- listen closely to the passage that is read to you,
- give thoughtful responses,
- apply all of your knowledge and skills to the tasks,
- carefully manage your time during the test, and
- do your very best.

WHAT ARE THE THREE BOOKS OF THE TEST?

The three books are Book 1: Reading, Book 2: Listening and Writing Mechanics, and Book 3: Reading and Writing. They test ELA Standards 1 through 3. Figure 1.2 shows the percentage of questions that assess each standard.

Standard 1. Reading, Writing, Listening, and Speaking for Information and Understanding	39%
Standard 2. Reading, Writing, Listening, and Speaking for Literary Response and Expression	39%
Standard 3. Reading, Writing, Listening, and Speaking for Critical Analysis and Evaluation	22%

Figure 1.2 Approximate Percentage of Questions Assessing Standards 1, 2, and 3. (Remember, Standard 4 is not assessed on this test.)

Each book is described fully in Chapters 4 and 5 of this review book. You will also have an opportunity at that time to practice answering sample questions. But first, here is a quick introduction to each book of the test.

Book 1: Reading has a number of passages for you to read on your own. Each passage is followed by a few multiple-choice questions about the passage. Your answers will show how well you understand the passages. They will show how well you can get information from, interpret, respond to, or critically analyze the passages. These passages may be fiction or nonfiction, poems or stories, or a variety of other types of reading. (See Appendix A for a list of literary genres.) The vocabulary and content are both relevant to what you have been reading in class and for homework. You will fill in circles on an answer sheet that is separate from your test book.

Book 2: Listening and Writing Mechanics has an article that will be read to you. You will listen to the article twice. You are encouraged to be an active listener and take notes as you listen closely to the article. Pages will be available in the test booklet for you to write your notes. You may refer to your notes as you answer the questions about the article. You will be asked to answer several multiple-choice and short-response questions. Place your answers to the multiple-choice questions on the separate answer sheet that will be provided, and write your short responses right in your test booklet. Multiple-choice questions about writing mechanics (spelling, punctuation, and grammar) are included in this book.

Book 3: Reading and Writing gives you two passages to read on your own and asks you to respond to five writing prompts to show that you understand the passages. You will show that you know how to read critically and that you know how to write in various genres, such as narrative, persuasive, and informative. You will respond to four short-response questions and one extended-response question, writing your responses directly in the test booklet.

HOW IS THE TEST SCORED?

Your answers on the ELA test will show if you

- understand what the passages mean,
- can use information from the passages to support ideas,
- can organize your ideas,
- can use language effectively and expressively,
- can read and write critically,
- can spell and punctuate correctly, and
- can use paragraphing and grammar correctly.

For up-to-date information on scoring, go to *www.nysed.gov*.

ONLINE RESOURCES

You will find these websites helpful to learn more about the setup of the Grade 7 ELA test and the ideas behind the state Learning Standards.

- To see a set of all the New York State Learning Standards, go to the New York State Education Department's website at *http://www.emsc.nysed.gov/ciai/standards.html*.
- To see the complete set of English Language Arts Learning Standards, go to *http://www.emsc.nysed.gov/ciai/ela/elarg.html*.
- To see more practice ELA tests, go to *www.nysedregents.org/testing/elaei/06exams/home.htm*.

CONGRATULATIONS!

Now you have a lot of information about the Grade 7 test. You know there are three books and what each book covers. Knowing all this in advance will help you feel more relaxed and confident on the test days. You aren't going into the test in complete darkness.

Now, continue on to Chapter 2, which is all about effective literacy strategies. Chapter 2 will provide ideas to help you read, write, edit, listen, and take notes better. You will be able to apply the strategies described in Chapter 2 not only to the Grade 7 ELA test but to all literacy experiences. These strategies will give you the tools you need to be a more literate person.

Chapter 2

EFFECTIVE LITERACY STRATEGIES

WHAT IS LITERACY?

At home and in school we read, write, listen, and speak all the time and for many purposes. Literacy is part of our everyday lives. Think about it! How often do you search the Internet, text a friend, read a magazine, talk about your favorite television shows or movies, and enjoy music lyrics and other creative arts? These are all examples of literacy. We are literate if we can understand others and communicate our thoughts and ideas. Literacy involves creating meaning from texts that we read and listen to and expressing ourselves through writing and speaking. The more we practice our literacy skills inside and outside of school, the better we become at them. When we are interested in and excited about engaging in literacy activities, like the ones described, we get better by trying out new things and experimenting.

WHAT ARE SOME EFFECTIVE LITERACY STRATEGIES?

In the following sections, we will share many strategies that will help you become more confident and skilled as a reader, writer, and listener. As you read through the following charts, check off how often you use these strategies when you read—always, sometimes, or never. Then, try using each of them—especially the ones you don't ordinarily use—in reading and responding to the sample passages in Chapters 4 through 6 and Practice Tests 1 and 2 in this book.

READING STRATEGIES

Before reading something, do you...

Always   Sometimes   Never

_____   _____   _____   Look over the title, any headings, pictures, and captions—the general structure of the text—to get an idea of what the piece is about?

_____   _____   _____   Skim through the piece to see how it is organized and how long it is?

_____   _____   _____   Think about what you already know or have read about the topic?

_____   _____   _____   Predict what you might learn from the piece or what the story might be about?

_____   _____   _____   Consider how the author's perspective might influence the way the passage is written?

While reading something, do you...

Always   Sometimes   Never

_____   _____   _____   Make the words and the story come alive by creating a movie in your mind? Visualize the characters and events? Ask yourself, Have I entered the world of the story?

_____   _____   _____   Ask yourself, Do I still understand what is going on here? Do I understand the characters, their motivation, the plot, the setting, the imagery, and so on? Can I summarize what has happened so far?

_____   _____   _____   Go back and reread from the place where you did understand to figure out what you missed the first time through?

_____   _____   _____   Ask yourself, What is the main idea here?

_____   _____   _____   Keep track of any clues and the supporting ideas?

_____   _____   _____   Make connections to what you know about the topic?

——— ——— ——— Ask yourself, What logical, safe predictions can I make about what is going to happen next?

——— ——— ——— Use clues from the piece to figure out vocabulary words you do not know?

——— ——— ——— Question the author's purpose and positions?

——— ——— ——— Question the reading genre and what that means about how you should interpret the piece? Figure out if you are reading facts, someone's opinions, fantasy, a tall tale, or something else? Follow the sequencing?

——— ——— ——— Highlight the most important points you want to remember, such as the who, what, when, where, how, and why of the story? Make brief notes in the margins?

After reading something, do you…

Always   Sometimes   Never

——— ——— ——— Think about the really important ideas and how they are connected to each other?

——— ——— ——— Try to figure out the main idea or purpose of the piece?

——— ——— ——— Try to "read between the lines" or think about possible hidden meanings or messages?

——— ——— ——— Figure out your feelings about the piece? Ask yourself, Did I like it or not? Why? Did it make me laugh or feel sad? Was it realistic and logical?

——— ——— ——— Ask yourself, How does this connect with what I already knew about the topic? How does it differ from or add to what I already knew?

——— ——— ——— Summarize the piece in your own words?

——— ——— ——— Check back to find information or details you don't recall?

WRITING STRATEGIES

Before writing do you...

Always	Sometimes	Never	
_____	_____	_____	Think about and plan what you will write?
_____	_____	_____	Think about what your reader will need to understand what you've written? What kinds of vocabulary words will you use? What important ideas and details must be included?
_____	_____	_____	Decide what type of language and grammar you will use? Will your writing be formal or informal? Who will read your piece?
_____	_____	_____	Decide what structure you will use in your writing? Paragraphs? Diagrams? Complete sentences? A form of poetry?
_____	_____	_____	Sketch out your overall plan in a visual way? Decide if you will use a graphic organizer or an outline to brainstorm and organize your ideas?
_____	_____	_____	Carefully read all of the headings in the graphic organizer? Study the structure of the graphic organizer to determine how it fits what you want to say and the information you have from the passage? Plan possible responses and where to place them in the graphic organizer? Think about how parts of your response fit together?
_____	_____	_____	Carefully read and reread the question to which you are going to respond, underlining the important parts of the question, such as how many examples or details you need, what you are supposed to describe or explain, and any other important requests?
_____	_____	_____	Think about how you will compose a comprehensive topic sentence to begin your response?

While writing do you...

Always   Sometimes   Never

_____   _____   _____   Write a rough draft just to get your ideas down first?

_____   _____   _____   Read and reread parts you have written as you add to the piece?

_____   _____   _____   Reread the question or prompt frequently to be sure you are focused and sticking to the task?

_____   _____   _____   Freely revise and move words, sentences, or paragraphs around to find clearer ways to say things?

_____   _____   _____   Ask yourself, How can I make this clearer or better organized?

_____   _____   _____   Add or delete information as needed, especially illuminating details from the passages? Evaluate your writing?

_____   _____   _____   Talk with someone about your writing to get feedback or ideas? (Of course, you can't do this during the state ELA test, but it's a great strategy to use when you are preparing for the test.)

After writing do you...

Always   Sometimes   Never

_____   _____   _____   Reread the question or prompt to be sure you've stuck to the task throughout the response?

_____   _____   _____   Read and reread what you wrote as if you were the reader? Listen to what you've written as if you're hearing it for the first time? Listen critically to see what you need to change, add, or cut out completely? Keep asking yourself, Does this answer the question or prompt, as you revise?

_____   _____   _____   Go back and look for places where you can substitute more effective or descriptive words for what you have?

_____   _____   _____   Read your piece through a final time _just_ to edit for spelling, punctuation, and grammatical errors?

_____   _____   _____   Check paragraphing and overall organization?

_____   _____   _____   Share your writing with someone to get feedback? (Of course, you can do this only when preparing for the state ELA test, not on the actual test days.)

EDITING STRATEGIES TO CHECK WRITING CONVENTIONS

When you are editing for the conventions of writing, such as spelling, grammar, and punctuation, do you...

Always	Sometimes	Never	
_____	_____	_____	Underline areas where you initially find mistakes, then reread your writing to check a second time?
_____	_____	_____	Ask yourself, What types of mistakes did I find? and then think about the grammatical/mechanical rule you will follow to fix each mistake?
_____	_____	_____	Correct each mistake by crossing out one word or phrase at a time and writing the correction above each?

When you are finished editing, do you...

Always	Sometimes	Never	
_____	_____	_____	Double-check for spelling errors?
_____	_____	_____	Double-check for capitalization errors (proper nouns, beginnings of sentences, beginnings of quotes)?
_____	_____	_____	Double-check for punctuation errors (periods, commas, apostrophes, quotation marks)?
_____	_____	_____	Double-check for syntax errors (order of phrases in a sentence)?
_____	_____	_____	Double-check for sentence fragments and/or run-on sentences?
_____	_____	_____	Double-check for proper word usage (correct pronouns, verb tense, and singular/plural verb use)?
_____	_____	_____	Double-check for the types of errors you consistently seem to make in your writing?

LISTENING AND NOTE-TAKING STRATEGIES

Before listening do you...

Always   Sometimes   Never

_____   _____   _____   Check the directions for key vocabulary words and definitions so that you understand them when you hear them?

_____   _____   _____   Decide what note-taking structure will work best for you (a t-chart, bullets, a timeline, an outline)?

While listening do you...

Always   Sometimes   Never

_____   _____   _____   Avoid physical distractions by looking right at the reader's face or mouth when you aren't taking notes?

_____   _____   _____   Take notes only on the key points instead of writing down every little detail?

_____   _____   _____   Use symbols, abbreviations, or drawings to save time during note-taking?

_____   _____   _____   Use X's to mark places where you missed key information the first time the passage is read?

After listening do you...

Always   Sometimes   Never

_____   _____   _____   Review your notes, adding details to any areas where you are missing important information?

PUTTING IT ALL TOGETHER

Now that you have examined the literacy strategies that can help you successfully complete each section of the test, it is time to start putting them into practice. When you begin working on a new sample passage, make sure you come back to this list of strategies and review the tips that will help you complete the questions successfully. The more you practice using them, the quicker they will become good habits!

ONLINE RESOURCES

These websites will help you learn about other literacy techniques that you can use to improve your comprehension.

- Adlit.org offers before-, during-, and after-reading strategies for parents and teachers to help improve students' comprehension, as well as downloadable graphic organizers for the strategies. Check it out at *www.adlit.org/strategy_library*.

- The Literacy and Learning site showcases four PDF handbooks that cover numerous literacy techniques. To preview the easy-to-follow, step-by-step format, go to *www.litandlearn.lpb.org/strategies.html*.

CONGRATULATIONS!

Now you have learned many strategies that will help you when you are

- reading,

- writing,

- editing, and

- listening and note-taking.

Make sure you return to these strategies and use them when you are completing the practice passages in Chapters 4 through 6 and the passages in Practice Tests 1 and 2.

EFFECTIVE TEST-TAKING STRATEGIES

THE RIGHT MINDSET

One of the most important things you can do for yourself before you take the New York State ELA test is to make sure that you have the right mindset. This means you should try not to panic or get nervous beforehand! Remember that you have done your best to prepare yourself for this assessment. Reading this book will help you make sure you understand what strategies will work best for every section of the test. Completing the practice tests and comparing your answers to those in the keys will make you familiar with the format of the test as well as how the state will assess your answers. On the day of the test, you will not have to worry about any surprises. You will already know everything you need to know about the test—the breakdown, the format, what strategies to use, what the state will be looking for in your answers, and how your answers will be graded. After you have read this book, practiced the strategies, completed the practice exercises, and reviewed your answers, you can be confident that you have taken all of the steps necessary to prepare yourself. All you will need to do then is to apply what you have learned to the actual test!

PREPARING FOR THE TEST

Preparing for the test means more than just practice, however. You also need to make sure your body is ready for test day. The first step is making sure you get a good night's sleep the night before the test. A good night's sleep will ensure that you are not overtired or sleepy during the timed sections of the assessment. If you go into the test with only a few hours of sleep, your mind is more likely to drift off while you are reading the test passages. It will be harder for you to focus during the listening portion of the test and to identify the most important points being made. It will be harder for you to organize your thoughts when answering short- and extended-response questions. Taking the test without getting enough sleep the night before will make it harder for your brain to work. Going to bed a little early the night before will allow your brain to get the rest it needs to work to its full potential.

Along with rest, your body and mind also need fuel. Eat a good breakfast before you go to school on test day. Food works just like sleep—it allows your brain to focus and keeps you alert during all portions of the test. Without breakfast, you are likely to become sleepy during the test because your body will burn any calories left from the food you ate the day before. Compare your body to a car. Without gasoline, a car won't run and may get stuck on the side of the road, unable to go any further. The driver may be able to push the car a little bit until getting to a gas station, but that will be very difficult. When you don't eat breakfast, your body is like a car with very little gas. It may work for a little while, but your brain will become sluggish and it will become more and more difficult to answer the test questions (just as it is difficult to push a car to a gas station). Don't run out of gas! Be prepared and make sure your tank is full—eat a good breakfast the morning of the test.

TEST DAY

Set your morning alarm! You certainly do not want to be late to school on the day of the test. Arriving to school on time will ease your anxiety. You will have time to get situated at your test site and make sure you have all the materials you need for the session. The test proctor will have your test booklets and answer keys for you. You need to make sure you bring at least two sharpened no. 2 pencils with you. Highlighters are also permitted; you may want to use one to highlight key points during the reading section of the test, or to help you organize your notes during the listening portion.

Here is a quick summary of the important things you want to do to prepare for this day:

1. Have a positive, confident attitude—study and practice have prepared you for this day. Remind yourself that you have prepared for this test and you are ready to be successful.

2. Get plenty of rest and eat a good breakfast. Proper rest and food will give your body and mind the strength they need to complete the test.

3. Arrive prepared and on time. Get to school on time so you don't feel rushed. Bring the pencils and highlighters you will need.

MONITORING TIME LIMITS

There are time limits for each section of this test, so it is very important that you pay attention to the start time and the finish time that will be announced by your test proctor. Split the time in half so you are aware of the halfway point for each section. You need to make sure that you budget your time wisely so that you can complete all of the questions by the time the proctor calls, "Time's up!"

Here is an example. In the reading section of the test, Book 1, you will be given about one hour to read eight or more reading passages and answer several multiple-choice questions for each passage. When the section begins, start off by reviewing how long the passages are and what types of and how many questions you need to complete. Divide the 41 questions in half, and keep an eye on the time. Try to have at least half of the questions completed by the halfway point.

However, this does not mean you should rush through the test! Rushing through the sections and not following the strategies that are outlined in this book will only lead to making more mistakes. Simply stay focused on the task at hand, but make sure you don't spend too much time laboring over individual questions. If you reach a question that you are having difficulty answering, skip over it and answer the questions that are easier. Circle the skipped question number on your answer sheet so you don't accidentally mismatch the questions and their answers. Just make sure you return to the skipped question later! You don't want to forget about it and leave it blank. Also, sometimes when you come back to a difficult problem, it seems much easier. Putting a couple of minutes between you and a tricky question can ease your anxiety and make the test flow more smoothly for you.

Also, if you finish a section of the test before your time is up, make sure you go back and review your answers. This is especially important for your short- and extended-response questions and graphic organizers. Review these answers for solid details, organization, proper grammar, and spelling and mechanical errors. You will not be penalized for finding mistakes in your writing and correcting them, so it is worthwhile to use any extra time to double-check your work.

Here is a quick list of what you need to do to make sure you monitor your time limits during the test:

1. Be aware of the start and finish time when they are announced. Make sure you know the halfway point for the section.

2. Keep an eye on the time as you answer questions. Do not spend too much time on difficult questions. Go on to other questions, and return to the problematic questions later.

3. Use extra time to check your work. If you finish before your time is up, go back and double-check your work for errors.

ANSWERING MULTIPLE-CHOICE QUESTIONS

Multiple-choice questions can be some of the easiest questions to answer and some of the hardest questions to answer. The key to successfully answering this type of question is knowing the strategies that will help you pick out the correct answer.

The first thing you should do with any multiple-choice question is to read it over and underline one or two key words in the question. For example, if a question contains the word *except*, you know you need to narrow your choices down to the one that is not true. If you see phrases like *similar* to or *different from*, you know the question is asking you to make a comparison. The phrase *main idea* is asking you to identify the big picture. Isolating key words and phrases such as these will help you narrow your choices.

Second, read over all of the choices. Even if you think choice A is the correct answer, read through all of them. Sometimes other choices also seem to be correct and you need to decide which one is *most* correct, or they are all correct and you need to select choice D, *all of the above*. While you are reading over the choices, cross out those that you immediately know are incorrect. This is called process of elimination, and it will make your final selection much easier because you will have fewer answers from which to choose.

Some questions you will be able to answer easily, whereas others will be more difficult. Answer the easy questions first, and then reread the passage. Search for key words or phrases that appear in both the question and the passage many times, Making these connections can help you locate the key section in the passage that contains the answer to the question.

When all else fails, take your best guess. This is your final strategy. Do not leave any answer blank. If you cannot figure out an answer, do not remain on it for too long. Make an intelligent guess, circle the question number for your reference, and then if you have additional time at the end of the section, go back to it.

Let's sum up the strategies you should use when answering multiple-choice questions:

1. Read over the question and underline one or two key words. Look for words and phrases that focus on what the question is asking, such as *except, similar to, different from,* or *main idea.*

2. Read over all of the choices and cross out the ones you immediately know are incorrect. This is the process of elimination, and it will make your final selection easier.

3. Answer the easy questions first. Once those are complete, go back and look for context clues to help you answer the more difficult questions.

4. Do not leave any questions blank. If you don't know the answer, take your best guess. If you leave the question blank, you will definitely get it wrong. If you make an intelligent guess, you have a one in four chance of getting it right.

ONLINE RESOURCES

Here are some great websites for learning more test preparation and test-taking strategies:

▪ *www.testtakingtips.com*

This site is broken into several different sections, including test-taking tips, study skills and tips, note-taking, reducing test anxiety, and test-taking tips for parents. You can simply click on each section for specific suggestions.

▪ *www.studygs.net*

This Study Guides and Strategies site does not limit itself to test-taking strategies. It also has helpful hints for time management and effective problem solving, reading, writing, and studying.

CONGRATULATIONS!

Now you know what strategies you will need to use to get ready to take the test and to complete the test successfully. You have learned strategies for

▪ making sure your body and mind are rested and fueled for test day,

▪ feeling confident and prepared on the day of the test,

▪ monitoring your time for each section of the test, and

▪ reviewing and answering multiple-choice questions.

Now, continue on to Chapter 4, where you will learn all about Book 1 of the state test.

BOOK 1: READING

DESCRIPTION

I n this chapter, we will take a look at Book 1, the reading section of the state test. In Book 1, you will be given a variety of passages to read. The passages will represent different types of literary genres, such as folk tales, fables, interviews, essays, and biographies, to name a few. (See Appendix A for a list of descriptions of relevant literary genres.) Your job will be to use your reading skills and apply the reading strategies you have learned in class and in this book (see Chapter 2) to construct meaning from the passages. You will demonstrate your understanding of the passages by responding to several reading comprehension questions.

Book 1 contains eight or more reading passages. Each passage is followed by several multiple-choice questions. All together, there are 41 multiple-choice questions.

You will be allowed 70 minutes to complete Book 1. That includes reading all of the passages and answering all of the questions. On the day of the test, your teacher will go over the directions with you in detail and show you how to mark your answers. In the next section we will highlight several key points to help you understand how to do your best. You want to demonstrate and be proud of all of the reading skills and strategies you have mastered so far. That's what this book is all about!

TEST DIRECTIONS

On the day of the test, you will be given a booklet that includes the passages and questions, along with a separate answer sheet on which you will mark your responses to the multiple-choice questions. Your teacher will carefully instruct you on how much time you will have, how and where to mark your answers, and so on. You will have many opportunities to ask the teacher questions if you don't understand the directions.

Here are some important points to remember.

KEY POINT #1: Answer the questions based on the passage, not on your personal experiences or opinions.

You will most likely know something about the topic in the passage. You might have a similar experience that relates to the passage, or you may have a strong opinion about an issue discussed in a passage. But remember that this is a *reading* test. When you answer the questions, use what you understand about the topic from reading, understanding, and interpreting the passage. Do not let your personal experiences or opinions influence your responses.

KEY POINT #2: You can look back at the passages any time you want to check something.

Read the entire passage first so you understand the whole meaning. Then, as you read through and answer the questions, scan or reread parts of the passage to find or verify your answers. Of course, since this is a timed test, you have to be careful not to use up an excessive amount of valuable time rereading. (See Chapter 3 for ideas on monitoring your time.)

KEY POINT #3: You may highlight or make other marks in the book.

While you are reading, you might decide you want to underline or highlight details, key phrases, or other important information. (See Chapter 2 for suggestions on highlighting effectively.) Many students find that highlighting as they read helps them store information and focus their attention. When you get to the questions, the highlighting you did while reading may help you quickly locate details in the passage. Or, you might want to jot down a few notes in the margins or cross out the incorrect multiple-choice responses as you eliminate them. Practice these strategies as you work through the passages in this book.

It is really important, though, to remember that your answers *must be marked on the answer sheet* to get credit for them. When marking your answers, take note of the following important directions.

- Clearly mark your answers on the answer sheet. You certainly don't want to lose points because the scorer can't tell which response you selected!

- Check and double-check that you have matched the test question number in the booklet to the number on the answer sheet.

- Use a no. 2 pencil to make a heavy, dark mark to fill in the circle for the letter matching your answer.

- Erase completely and re-mark your answer sheet if you decide to change any of your answers.

- Avoid making any stray marks on the answer sheet that might be mistaken for an answer.

Practice these tips for marking the answer sheet when you do the practice tests at the end of this book.

TESTING ACCOMMODATIONS

Students with an Individualized Education Program (IEP) or Section 504 Accommodation Plan generally will be allowed their normal testing accommodations when completing Book 1, EXCEPT that only the directions—no other part of Book 1—may be read aloud to the student.

A few days before the test, ask your teacher what accommodations you will be allowed during the test so you know what to expect.

BREAKDOWN OF QUESTIONS

Through your responses to the questions in Book 1, your teachers and you will begin to understand your reading abilities based on New York State Learning Standards 1, 2, and 3. That is, when you read, how well can you

Standard 1. Collect and use data, facts, and ideas?
Discover relationships, concepts, and generalizations?

Standard 2. Relate texts to your own life?
Interpret meanings from texts?

Standard 3. Analyze and evaluate experiences, ideas, information, and issues presented by others?

GETTING STARTED

Are you ready to dig in and get started? Great! The first thing to do is think about what you already do when you are asked to respond to a text. You want to build on strategies that you already find useful. For example, when you don't know the meaning of a word, do you use the words and paragraphs around the word to help you figure out what the unknown word means? Do you use context clues? That is an excellent strategy to use!

Now, in a few words, describe how you would begin to:

1. Predict what is going to happen next in a story. _____

_____

2. Identify an author's point of view. _____

_____

3. Interpret a character's motivation. _____

_____

Review the reading strategies in Chapter 2. The charts include strategies for collecting, interpreting, analyzing, and evaluating passages. Now is your chance to apply these strategies, along with others you may know and use, to the sample passages and questions that follow. Here's how.

First, read the entire passage using the before-reading and during-reading strategies described in Chapter 2. Then, begin to answer each question. After you read each question, ask yourself,

Is the question asking me to collect, interpret, or analyze information?

Then, think about what strategy or strategies you should use to answer the question. For example, if the question is asking you to collect information, you might choose to look back into the passage. Once you locate the information you need, you may still need to use context clues to figure out the answer.

As you work your way through the questions, jot down the reading strategies you used in the spaces provided after each question. (See Chapter 2.) You may want to jot down other strategies you used, too, such as how you narrowed down the multiple-choice options. This will help you remember the strategies that are available, and soon they will automatically pop into your head when you need them.

SAMPLE QUESTIONS WITH GUIDED PRACTICE

As you work through the guided practices in this chapter, read the directions and each passage carefully. You will practice answering multiple-choice and short-response questions similar to those on the tests. This practice will help you improve your literacy skills.

SAMPLE PASSAGE A

Directions: Read this passage about how writers sometimes predict the future in their writing. Then answer questions 1 through 3.

PREDICTING THE FUTURE?

Elaine Lawrence

Writers of the past sometimes predicted the future. They wrote books, short stories, and television shows that included ideas that some people thought were unbelievable. But surprisingly, some of those ideas actually did come to pass.

When looking at the work of many science fiction, or sci-fi, writers, we find a broad range of talents. The list includes writers of the distant past, such as Jules Verne and H. G. Wells, as well as more recent writers, such as Ray Bradbury and Isaac Asimov. In fact, the list of writers who wrote about future events could fill volumes.

In the late 1800s, Jules Verne and H. G. Wells showed great foresight in their predictions about technological advances. Verne accurately predicted large submarines that could dive to the ocean floor. Today, the Navy uses some of the same types of submersibles about which Verne wrote. Wells accurately predicted the atomic bomb long before the first atomic bomb was created and used. Both Ray Bradbury and Isaac Asimov wrote stories in the 1950s and 1960s about humanlike robots (androids) who would walk among humans by the twenty-first century. Today the Honda Corporation has a humanlike robot that can serve people beverages and engage them in social conversations. The robot's name is Asimo, which is very similar to Asimov.

Predictions made by more recent writers are of high interest to us because these predictions seem to have only recently occurred. For instance, the sci-fi series *Star Trek* was first written and televised in 1966. The original writer of the show, Gene Roddenberry, depicted desktop-type computers being used

Asimo, Honda Corporation's humanlike robot

everywhere "in the future." He also described "communicators" that looked very much like a common device in today's world—the cell phone.

There doesn't appear to be one single method that each writer used to successfully make accurate predictions. We can only guess that they must have done their research and had phenomenal imaginations. While not all writers' predictions have come true, there is no doubt those that have were created by insightful and gifted writers.

1. According to the author, the idea that historically writers have predicted the technology of the future is

   A. nonsense

   B. surprising

   C. dreadful

   D. eerie

   Strategies you used: _____

   _____

2. Which detail **best** supports the main idea of the article?

   A. Gene Roddenberry predicted communicators like the cell phone would be developed in the future.

   B. The atomic bomb has been used only once in the history of the world.

   C. It is more interesting to think about recent predictions than it is to think about those that were made at the turn of the century.

   D. Science fiction writers have to do research to determine how technology will develop in the future.

   Strategies you used: _____

   _____

3. Which statement would the author say is **most likely** true of science fiction writers?

   A. Technological progress would be stunted were it not for the predictions of science fiction writers.

   B. Scientists often consult science fiction for technology ideas.

   C. Science fiction writers play an important role in shaping the technology of the future.

   D. In their writing, science fiction writers often accurately predict the types of technology that develop in the future.

Strategies you used: _____

_____

SAMPLE PASSAGE B

Directions: Read this passage from *Little Women* by Louisa May Alcott. Then answer questions 1 through 3.

---

drafted—to be selected for and required to join the military services

simper—to smile in a silly manner, to smirk

As they gathered about the table, Mrs. March said, with a particularly happy face, "I've got a treat for you after supper."

A quick, bright smile went round like a streak of sunshine. Beth clapped her hands, regardless of the biscuit she held, and Jo tossed up her napkin, crying, "A letter! A letter! Three cheers for Father!"

"Yes, a nice long letter. He is well, and thinks he shall get through the cold season better than we feared. He sends all sorts of loving wishes for Christmas, and an especial message to you girls," said Mrs. March, patting her pocket as if she had got a treasure there.

"Hurry and get done! Don't stop to quirk your little finger and simper over your plate, Amy," cried Jo, choking on her tea and dropping her bread, butter side down, on the carpet in her haste to get at the treat.

Beth ate no more, but crept away to sit in her shadowy corner and brood over the delight to come, till the others were ready.

"I think it was so splendid of Father to go as chaplain when he was too old to be drafted, and not strong enough for a soldier," said Meg warmly.

"Don't I wish I could go as a drummer, a vivan—what's its name? Or a nurse, so I could be near him and help him," exclaimed Jo, with a groan.

"It must be very disagreeable to sleep in a tent, and eat all sorts of bad-tasting things, and drink out of a tin mug," sighed Amy.

"When will he come home, Marmee?" asked Beth, with a little quiver in her voice.

"Not for many months, dear, unless he is sick. He will stay and do his work faithfully as long as he can, and we won't ask for him back a minute sooner than he can be spared. Now come and hear the letter."

They all drew to the fire, Mother in the big chair with Beth at her feet, Meg and Amy perched on either arm of the chair, and Jo leaning on the back, where no one would see any sign of emotion if the letter should happen to be touching. Very few letters were written in those hard times that were not touching, especially those which fathers sent home. In this one little was said of the hardships endured, the dangers faced, or the homesickness conquered. It was a cheerful, hopeful letter, full of lively descriptions of camp life, marches, and military news, and only at the end did the writer's heart over-flow with fatherly love and longing for the little girls at home.

Give them all of my dear love and a kiss. Tell them I think of them by day, pray for them by night, and find my best comfort in their affection at all times. A year seems very long to wait before I see them, but remind them that while we wait we may all work, so that these hard days need not be wasted. I know they will remember all I said to them, that they will be loving children to you, will do their duty faithfully, fight their bosom enemies bravely, and conquer themselves so beautifully that when I come back to them I may be fonder and prouder than ever of my little women.

Everybody sniffed when they came to that part. Jo wasn't ashamed of the great tear that dropped off the end of her nose, and Amy never minded the rumpling of her curls as she hid her face on her mother's shoulder and sobbed out, "I am a selfish girl! But I'll truly try to be better, so he mayn't be disappointed in me by-and-by."

"We all will," cried Meg. "I think too much of my looks and hate to work, but won't any more, if I can help it."

"I'll try and be what he loves to call me, 'a little woman,' and not be rough and wild, but do my duty here instead of wanting to be somewhere else," said Jo, thinking that keeping her temper at home was a much harder task than facing a rebel or two down South.

Beth said nothing, but wiped away her tears with the blue army sock and began to knit with all her might, losing no time in doing the duty that lay nearest her, while she resolved in her quiet little soul to be all that Father hoped to find her when the year brought round the happy coming home.

1. Read the statement below that is made by Jo:

   Don't I wish I could go as a drummer, a vivan—what's its name?

   What can the reader infer based on this statement?

   A. Jo was a shy young girl.

   B. Father was a drummer.

   C. The army that Father marched with had a band.

   D. The war being fought was not a modern war.

   Strategies you used: _____

   _____

2. Which girl acts the **most** impatient about wanting to hear her father's letter?

   A. Jo

   B. Meg

   C. Amy

   D. Beth

   Strategies you used: _____

   _____

3. Read this sentence from the passage:

   "Don't stop to quirk your little finger and simper over your plate, Amy."

   In this sentence, Jo means that

   A. Amy should stop pointing and staring at Jo

   B. Amy should not speak while she is eating

   C. Amy should not waste time trying to eat politely

   D. Amy should eat more politely and slowly

   Strategies you used: _____

   _____

SAMPLE PASSAGE C

Directions: Read this passage about ferrets. Then answer questions 1 through 3.

FERRETS, LARGELY MISUNDERSTOOD

Ann Morris

Many people have been misinformed about the modern-day domesticated ferret. It is a pet that is highly stigmatized as being vicious, foul-smelling, and untrainable. Ferrets are outlawed in Hawaii and California as well as some major cites because of these and many other misconceptions. Ferrets can make wonderful pets, but before buying one there are a few things that you should know.

Historically, ferrets were speculated to have been domesticated 2,500 years ago, around the same time as cats. Ferrets were primarily used in ferreting, which is the use of ferrets to hunt for small burrowing animals like rabbits. They were also used to protect grain in feed stores from mice and rats. They were even kept as companions in some cases by wealthy nobility.

Ferrets are not rodents. They are members of the Mustelidae family. This is a large group of mammals with scent glands under their tails. Weasels, mink, polecats, skunks, badgers, and wolverines are all in the Mustelidae family. Domestic ferrets are most closely related to the European polecat.

Ferrets can make very good pets if their scent glands are removed. They can be taught to do tricks and to use a litter box. What makes them stand out among other pets is a behavior they have when they are very happy. This behavior is known as the "weasel war dance" or the "popcorn dance," as ferret owners lovingly call it. The animals hop in the air on all fours and fling their bodies around, falling off and running into things in the process. They sleep 18 to 20 hours a day. Although they can be kept in a cage while sleeping, they do need a lot of play time outside the cage when awake or they can become depressed. They are bright, curious, and constantly seeking new items to hide away in their "stash." Despite misconceptions, ferrets, like dogs, will only bite if not taught otherwise.

Ferrets are just as sweet and friendly as any other well-trained pet. They are not the mean, snippy animals they are sometimes made out to be. Just as with any other pet, if you treat them with love and respect, they'll turn into wonderful companions.

1. This passage would be of **most** interest to a person who

    A. likes to read about animals

    B. is thinking of adopting a ferret as a pet

    C. wants to learn how ferrets dance

    D. needs information about the Mustelidae family

    Strategies you used: _____

    _____

2. Why did the author **most likely** include information about the historic uses of ferrets?

    A. to support the idea that ferrets are useful and trainable

    B. to show that ferrets have been around a long time

    C. to explain why you should get one instead of a cat

    D. to convince readers to get one for protection

    Strategies you used: _____

    _____

3. According to the passage, how is a ferret like a polecat?

    A. They both do the weasel war dance.

    B. They both can be trained.

    C. They both have scent glands under their tails.

    D. They both make good pets when trained well.

    Strategies you used: _____

    _____

Answers are on page 116.

ONLINE RESOURCES

Here are some great websites for learning more reading strategies:

■ *www.readingrockets.org/helping/target/comprehension#do_kids*

This site gives reading tips for students, parents, and teachers. Find out how to help yourself with reading comprehension under the "What Kids Can Do to Help Themselves" heading.

■ *www.learner.org/jnorth/tm/ReadStrats_20Best.html*

On this site you'll find 20 thinking strategies readers use to understand nonfiction texts. You'll learn tips for summarizing, finding the main idea, comparing texts, and lots more.

CONGRATULATIONS!

Now you know what Book 1 is all about. You have learned about its composition, directions, and breakdown. You have also learned strategies for

■ collecting information,

■ interpreting information, and

■ analyzing and evaluating information.

And, you learned all of this while you practiced sample questions like those found on the state tests! Next, continue on to Chapter 5, where you will learn all about Book 2 of the state test.

Chapter
5

BOOK 2: LISTENING AND WRITING MECHANICS

DESCRIPTION

In this chapter, we will take a look at Book 2, the listening and writing mechanics section of the state test. In Book 2 you will listen to a passage as it is read aloud. The passage may be taken from various literary genres, such as interviews, biographies, short stories, or essays, to name a few. (See Appendix A for a list of descriptions of relevant literary genres.) Your job is to use your listening skills to construct meaning from the passage. Based on your understanding of the readings and your knowledge and understanding of proper grammar, punctuation, and word usage, you will respond to various listening comprehension questions.

Book 2 contains one listening passage. The passage will be read out loud twice. You are allowed to take notes on the passage any time you wish. The passage will be followed by eight multiple-choice questions. After these questions, you may be asked to complete a graphic organizer and briefly respond in writing to one or two questions. You will be allowed 30 minutes after the second reading of the passage is complete to answer the listening questions.

TEST DIRECTIONS

You will be given a booklet and an answer sheet on which you will mark your responses to the multiple-choice questions. All graphic organizers and short-response questions will be completed inside the test booklet. Before the test begins, your teacher will tell you how much time you will have to complete Book 2, as well as how and where to put all of your answers. You will be able to ask questions if you do not understand the directions.

The test booklet will contain tips for taking the test. These are important reminders that can help you to stay focused when answering the test questions. Here are some of the tips.

- Read all directions carefully.

- Plan your time.

- Follow the steps of the writing process when answering written questions.

Following these suggestions can help you earn the most points possible for this section of the test.

There are some other important points that will help you be successful on this section of the test. Take note of the following.

KEY POINT #1: Take notes during both readings of the listening passage.

By taking notes both times the passage is read, you can add information that you may have missed during the first reading. While reviewing your notes during the second reading, you can add names, dates, places, or other critical details that you did not catch the first time. This will give you more material to draw from when answering the comprehension questions that follow.

KEY POINT #2: You can look back at your notes any time you want to check something.

You do not have to rely on your memory when answering any of the multiple-choice or short-response questions in this section. You can go back to your notes whenever you want to double-check your answers or to find extra details to support your written responses. (See Chapter 3 for ideas on answering multiple-choice and written response questions.)

KEY POINT #3: When you are finished, double-check your answers and proofread all of your work.

A large portion of your points for this section of the test will be earned based on your ability to proofread and edit written pieces. Famous authors review and revise their work before it gets published. Follow their example!

BREAKDOWN OF QUESTIONS

Book 2 focuses mainly on Standard 2 of the New York State English Language Arts Standards. It checks to see if you are able to read, write, and listen for literary response and expression.

GETTING STARTED

Before you begin practice activities for this section, review the writing, editing, listening and note-taking strategies that were outlined in Chapter 2. While you complete the practice activities, try using the new strategies that you did not check off and see how they help you. The answers to the sample questions are in Appendix C.

SAMPLE QUESTIONS WITH GUIDED PRACTICE

This section contains a practice listening passage, so you will need some help. Ask a skillful reader to assist you by reading the directions and passage to you.

> *Note to Reader:* Take the directions and the story "A Canadian Hero" out of the book by cutting on the perforation marks. That way, the student can use the note pages to take notes in the book while you read the directions and the passage twice.

The reader should first practice reading the story on his or her own and then read the selection to you *twice*. When the person reads, he or she should begin with the title and the name of the author. Then, the reader should read the selection at a steady and moderate pace—not too fast and not too slowly. The reader should speak in a clear voice and read with expression. Remember, the selection should be read two times. Each reading should take about five minutes.

> *From the Sideline: As you work through this guided practice, check these "From the Sideline" features to monitor your thinking. Use the strategies in these features as a guide to help you answer each question successfully. Check off each item as you monitor it.*

Directions: You will hear a biography called "A Canadian Hero" by Melissa Wadsworth-Miller. You will listen to the biography two times. You may take notes at any time as you listen to the story. Then you will use your notes to help you answer the questions that follow. Your answers to these questions will show your understanding of the biography.

Here are some words you will need to know as you listen to the passage:

- mediocre—ordinary; second-rate

- stamina—energy

A CANADIAN HERO

Melissa Wadsworth-Miller

On July 28, 1958, Terry Fox was born in Winnipeg, Manitoba, Canada. Terry proved to be a very active child who loved all kinds of sports, including soccer, rugby, baseball, and diving. However, he was not very tall; this forced him to work twice as hard as the bigger kids. Although this difficulty would have caused many to give up, it only made Terry try harder. This sense of determination is what motivated him throughout his life, and it is one of the reasons he is known as a Canadian hero.

When Terry was in junior high school, he loved basketball and wanted to play guard on his school's basketball team. However, because he was only five feet tall and mediocre at the game, many of his classmates thought he didn't stand a chance. Terry wasn't about to give up. Every day he would practice basketball, and by grade ten, he was one of the best guards on the team. Because of his persistence and determination, Terry achieved his goal. He carried this determination with him to the school's swim team, where he won numerous medals in swimming and diving. Many people were impressed with his stamina and endurance. These qualities would help him in his battle against cancer.

At age 18, Terry was diagnosed with bone cancer in his right leg. In order to prevent its spread, doctors had to amputate his leg several inches above his knee. No one would have judged Terry if he had decided to stop participating in sports after this life-changing surgery. However, once Terry recovered from his surgery and learned how to use his artificial leg, he decided to run from coast to coast in order to raise money for cancer research. He called his run The Marathon of Hope, and his goal was to raise $1 from each Canadian citizen. When he reflected on his cancer treatment, he stated, "I remember promising myself that, should I live, I would rise up to meet this new challenge face to face and prove myself worthy of life, something too many people take for granted."

At the beginning of Terry's marathon on April 12, 1980, he dipped his artificial leg in the Atlantic Ocean at St. John's, Newfoundland. He intended to dip it again in the Pacific Ocean at Vancouver, British Columbia. Terry ran an average of 23.3 miles a day, roughly the distance of a typical marathon, and he kept this pace for 143 days. People would line the streets of the towns he ran through in order to cheer him on.

Unfortunately, Terry was unable to finish his run. On September 1, Terry was forced to stop his marathon when it was discovered that his cancer had spread to his lungs. He had run a total of 3,339 miles through several provinces in Canada.

Terry Fox died several months afterward, at the age of 22. But his Marathon of Hope had captured Canada's attention. A nationwide telethon was organized in the hope of raising additional funds for cancer research. This and other fundraising campaigns were so successful that by February 1981, $24.17 million dollars had been raised. Terry Fox's dream of getting one dollar from every single Canadian for cancer research had been fulfilled.

Because of Terry Fox's strength in the face of adversity and his desire to help others, he is considered a national hero of Canada. In his memory, Terry Fox Run events are organized all across Canada, the United States, and in other countries around the world, and they have raised countless millions for cancer research. The Terry Fox Monument still stands in Thunder Bay, Canada, near where his Marathon of Hope ended.

NOTES

NOTES

Strategies you used for listening: _____

_____

Strategies you used for taking notes: _____

_____

Multiple-Choice Questions

> *From the Sideline:* Tips for the Multiple-Choice Questions
> ■ *What is each question asking? Underline phrases in each question that help you focus on the specific information needed.*
> ■ *Think about the answer before choosing your response.*
> ■ *Check your notes to see if you have details from the passage to support your answer.*

1. When he was a child, what physical trait made Terry Fox have to work harder at sports?

   A. his stamina

   B. his height

   C. his determination

   D. his artificial leg

Strategies you used: _____

2. Terry Fox set all of the following goals for himself except

   A. completing the Marathon of Hope

   B. playing guard on his school's basketball team

   C. raising $1 from each Canadian citizen for cancer research

   D. becoming a national hero

Strategies you used: _____

3. Terry Fox's attitude can best be described as

   A. unwavering

   B. anxious

   C. negative

   D. content

Strategies you used: _____

4. The main purpose of this article is to

   A. entertain

   B. persuade

   C. inform

   D. compare

Strategies you used: _____

5. Read the following quote:

   The Terry Fox Monument still stands in Thunder Bay, Canada.

   Why is the Terry Fox Monument capitalized?

   A. It is a pronoun.

   B. It is a contraction.

   C. It is a predicate.

   D. It is a proper noun.

Strategies you used: _____

6. Which of the following sentences uses the correct punctuation?

   A. However, he was not very tall; this forced him to work twice as hard as the bigger kids.

   B. However he was not very tall this forced him to work twice as hard as the bigger kids.

   C. However; he was not very tall. This forced him to work twice as hard as the bigger kids.

   D. However, he was not very tall, this forced him to work twice as hard as the bigger kids.

Strategies you used: _____

7. Read the following quote:

   Terry wasn't about to give up.

   An apostrophe is used in the word wasn't because it is a

   A. compound word

   B. conjunction

   C. contraction

   D. complex word

Strategies you used: _____

8. Read the following quote:

   Terry proved to be a very active child who loved all kinds of sports, including soccer rugby baseball and diving.

   What corrections need to be made to the quote?

   A. The names of all the sports need to be capitalized.

   B. A period needs to go after *child* and the word *who* needs to be capitalized.

   C. The period at the end of the sentence needs to be changed to an exclamation point.

   D. Commas need to be placed after the words *sports, soccer, rugby,* and *baseball.*

   Strategies you used: _____

Short-Response Questions

9. One of Terry Fox's character traits was a strong sense of determination. Complete the chart below using details from the passage to describe three obstacles or challenges Terry faced in his life. Also, explain how his determination helped him overcome the obstacle or challenge.

   > *From the Sideline: What is the question asking?*
   > ▪ *Underline phrases that focus in on what you should include in your answer.*

Obstacles or Challenges Terry Faced	How Terry Overcame the Obstacles or Challenges

   > *From the Sideline: In your answer, be sure you*
   > ▪ *fully describe the obstacle with details from the story, and*
   > ▪ *include details to explain how determination helped Terry overcome these problems.*

   Strategies you used: _____

10. The end of the passage states:

Because of Terry Fox's strength in the face of adversity and his desire to help others, he is considered a national hero of Canada.

What did Terry Fox do to show he was committed to helping others? How did his determination motivate him during his personal difficulties? Use details from the passage to support your answer.

> *From the Sideline: What is the question asking?*
> ■ *Underline phrases that focus in on what you should include in your answer.*

_____

_____

_____

_____

_____

_____

> *From the Sideline: Be sure your answer*
> ■ *uses details from the passage to describe Terry Fox's efforts to help others, and*
> ■ *explains the personal difficulties Terry faced and describes why he was determined **not** to give up on his goal.*

Strategies you used: _____

11. Although Terry Fox has passed away, the reader can infer that he inspired others to follow his lead. What details from the passage can be used to infer that others are continuing Terry Fox's mission? Use details from the passage to support your answer.

_____

_____

_____

_____

_____

> *From the Sideline:* Be sure your answer
> - *clearly states your inference at the beginning of your answer, and*
> - *uses details from the passage to support your inference.*

Strategies you used: _____

Answers are on pages 117–123.

ONLINE RESOURCES

You will find these websites helpful to learn more about listening and editing skills.

- Find out what it means to really listen, and get tips for being a good listener at *www.infoplease.com/homework/listeningskills1.html.*

- This fabulous eMINTS website for teachers offers games, tons of links to learn about editing and proofreading, and opportunities to practice your skills. Check it out at *www.emints.org/ethemes/ resources/S00001517.shtml.*

CONGRATULATIONS!

Now you know what Book 2 is all about. You have read about the parts of the test, the test directions, and the question breakdown. As you completed the sample questions, you also practiced a number of strategies for

- listening and note-taking,

- completing multiple-choice questions,

- completing short-response and graphic organizer questions, and

- proofreading and editing.

Now, move on to Chapter 6 to learn all about Book 3 of the seventh-grade test.

BOOK 3: READING AND WRITING

DESCRIPTION

In this chapter, we will take a look at Book 3, the reading and writing section of the state test. In Book 3, you will be given two passages to read. The passages may include short stories, poems, reports, how-to pieces, interviews, essays, newspaper articles, or any type of literary genre. (See Appendix A for a list of descriptions of relevant literary genres.) The passages will be followed by a number of writing prompts. You will be required to show that you know how to read critically and that you know how to write narrative, persuasive, and informative genres; and, you will be expected to write for several different types of audiences. For example, you might be writing to inform your classmates of a new cell phone's capabilities. Or, you may be writing to persuade your representative in Congress to vote in favor of a particular bill. You may even be asked to write a narrative describing to your teacher how you solved a particular problem you were having. Your written responses will be assessed based on how well your writing addresses the prompt and how well you show that you were able to understand and critically analyze the passages.

Your job will be to use your critical reading and writing skills and to apply the strategies you have learned in class and in this book (see Chapter 2) to read the passages, interpret the writing prompts, and construct clearly written responses. You will demonstrate your reading and writing skills by responding to four short-response questions and one extended-response question. To enable you to practice the skills you will be asked to demonstrate in Book 3, in this chapter we will guide you to:

■ Critically read a passage and answer two short-response questions about it;

■ Critically read a second passage and answer two short-response questions about it; and

■ Write an extended response to a final question that asks you to evaluate, compare, or contrast the two passages.

You may be asked to complete a graphic organizer of some kind about a passage. You have most likely constructed t-charts and webs before to help you organize your thoughts. (See the Online Resources section of this chapter for examples of several kinds of graphic organizers.) The graphic organizer commonly used on state tests in the past has been the t-chart, which helps you organize events or ideas into categories. See Figures 6.1 and 6.2.

Advantages of Mall Curfews	Disadvantages of Mall Curfews
Teens are supervised by adults	Teens lose independence
Fewer crimes in malls	Stereotyping of teens as problematic

Figure 6.1 A Two-Category T-Chart

Type of Animal	Habitat	How Habitat Protects
Lion	Jungle	Provides coverage
Chipmunk	Underground (holes)	Provides safety from predators

Figure 6.2 A Three-Category T-Chart

The extended-response question may require you to read two passages and write a critical response to them. You may be asked to compare what is similar in the articles and contrast what is different or to interpret and analyze information from both passages. Support your responses with details from both passages to show that you understand them. The question may also ask you to add your opinions and personal experiences to show your critical analysis skills. Your answers will show what you understand about the passages, but the questions may also require you to express your opinion, ideas, and thoughts as you critically analyze, compare, and contrast the readings. Critical analysis involves judging or expressing an opinion about what you have read. Your opinions and judgments should be based on details from the reading as they relate to your personal experiences.

On the day of the test, your teacher will go over the directions with you in detail. Then, you will be allowed approximately 60 minutes to read the passages and respond to the writing prompts. During that time, you will work independently—without help and without speaking to your classmates. At any time during your writing, you may look back to reread the passages and the writing prompts.

Your responses will be scored on how well you demonstrated your ability to

- Organize your writing in a way that clearly expresses what you learned;

- Logically and fully respond to the questions;

- Support your responses with several examples from the readings and, in the case of the extended-response question, reflect your personal experiences or opinions if they are asked for; and

- Use correct writing mechanics.

In the next section, we will highlight several key points to help you understand how to do your best. You want to demonstrate and be proud of all of the reading and writing skills and strategies you have mastered so far.

TEST DIRECTIONS

On the day of the test, your teacher will pass out Book 3. Using a no. 2 pencil, you will write your responses directly in the book. You may print or write in cursive. Whichever you choose, be sure it is clear and easy to read. Your teacher will carefully instruct you on how much time you will have, how and where to write your answers, and so on. You will have many opportunities to ask questions if you don't understand the directions.

Here are a few important points to remember for Book 3:

KEY POINT #1: For the extended-response question,
use the writing process.

Plan your writing, write your full draft, then go back and make revisions and edits. End with a final read-through as you proofread everything. Keep in mind that an hour can go by very quickly when you are writing, so it's important to spend some time planning. The work you do during this time will guide you as you move through your extended response. It will keep you on track so your thoughts don't begin to wander and take your writing off course. That can happen easily when you write, especially when you are feeling stressed. Use your most reliable prewriting strategy, whether it be to construct an outline, jot notes, or create a graphic organizer. Once you have a plan, write a first draft. You won't have time to write a second or final draft, so when you make revisions and edits, carefully erase words or sentences you want to change. You might want to use some proofreading symbols to insert words or sentences here and there or to move a sentence from one spot to another. Whatever you do, be sure to be clear and neat.

KEY POINT #2: Be sure to organize your hour
so you have enough time.

Within the hour you are given, you will have to read two passages and write several responses. As you practice Book 3 with the sample questions in this chapter and in the practice tests, note about how long each of these tasks takes you. Below is a suggested timeline for the tasks, but you should adjust the times to fit your personal needs. For example, maybe you will discover after taking the diagnostic test that if you invest a couple of extra minutes planning the extended response, it takes you less time to actually draft the response. Adjust the times to fit the way you work best. Here is a sample timeline:

Skimming over the writing prompts to focus your reading	2 minutes
Carefully reading and, when needed, rereading the passages or parts of them	15 minutes
Carefully reading and writing the four short responses	10 minutes
Planning the extended response	3 minutes
Drafting the extended response	20 minutes
Revising and editing the extended response	8 minutes
Taking a final look at all of the responses	2 minutes
	60 minutes

Basically, if you spend 30 minutes reading and planning and then 30 minutes writing and checking everything, your hour will be up. Of course, you won't sit there timing yourself with the clock every minute! But, you should have a ballpark idea of the sequence of steps you'll take and about how much time you will spend on each step of the process.

> KEY POINT #3: Pull details from the passages to support your responses. In the extended response, if asked, use examples from the passages to support your opinion, evaluation, and personal experiences with the topics.

Skim over the writing prompts *before* you start to read the passages. This strategy will help you focus on specific details to look for as you read the passages. While you're reading and rereading the passages, draw a star by phrases that might support how you're going to respond to the prompts. Then, carefully reread the writing prompts that follow the passages and think about how you might answer them using the phrases you starred during your read-through. As you begin to write, show that you understand the passages by pulling from the passages several ideas and details that support your responses. Use examples to show why you are saying what you say. Tell which parts of what the authors wrote inspired you to come up with the interpretations or conclusions you did.

When you answer the extended-response question, note that the question may require you to base your responses not only on the information in the passages you read but also on your personal experiences, opinions, and evaluation of the topic and passages. That is what makes this response *critical*. You aren't just pulling information from the passages, but you are showing how you personally understand and connect with the topic. You will not be scored on whether the scorer thinks your personal opinion is right or wrong but on how well you express your opinion. Read the question carefully to determine if it is asking you to intersperse your personal thoughts.

These key points are very important to do well on this part of the test.

TESTING ACCOMMODATIONS

Students with an Individualized Education Program (IEP) or Section 504 Accommodation Plan generally will be allowed their normal testing accommodations. Some exceptions may apply, however. A few days before the test, ask your teacher what accommodations you will be allowed during the test so you know what to expect.

BREAKDOWN OF QUESTIONS

The questions in Book 3 are based on ELA Standard 3 on critical analysis and evaluation. That is, when you read and write, how well can you analyze and evaluate experiences, ideas, information, and issues presented by others?

GETTING STARTED

Next, you will learn and practice strategies for critically analyzing and evaluating passages. To start, ask yourself

How do I already analyze or form judgments about what I read?

What do I already know about writing, especially writing critically?

Start with what you know and what already works for you. Then, review the reading and writing strategies in Chapter 2. The charts include strategies for interpreting, analyzing, and evaluating passages. Here's another chance for you to apply these strategies, along with those you already know and use. Answers to the sample questions are in Appendix C.

SAMPLE QUESTIONS WITH GUIDED PRACTICE

From the sideline: As you work through this guided practice, check the "From the Sideline" features to monitor your thinking. Use the strategies in these features as guides to help you answer each question successfully. Check off each item as you monitor it.

Directions: In Book 3 you will read two articles. You will write answers to five questions based on your reading. You may look back at the articles as frequently as you want.

> *From the sideline: Preview the passages and writing prompts using these before-reading strategies:*
> - *Look over the title, pictures, and overall structure to see what they're about.*
> - *Skim through to see how they are organized.*
> - *Think about what you already know about the topics.*
> - *Make predictions.*
> - *Consider the authors' perspectives.*
> - *Skim over the writing prompts and questions that follow the passage to focus your purpose for reading. Determine if you are being asked to insert your personal experiences and opinion or not.*

EXCERPT FROM *FREE FROM SCHOOL*

Rahul Alvares

You must try to understand that when I finished school I was as raw as raw could be. I had never traveled anywhere on my own, never purchased a train ticket, since like most kids my age I had only travelled with my parents or relatives and they made all the decisions. I had no experience of how to handle money (my knowledge being limited to spending the 50 paise or one rupee I would receive as pocket money now and then).

So while I had set my sights on travelling far and wide my parents wisely thought that I should begin by learning to manage on my own within Goa itself. It was also the rainy season and travelling around the country would be much more difficult they explained.

So I started out by helping at an aquarium shop in Mapusa, the town nearest my village. The proprietor of the shop is Ashok D'Cruz, a college friend of my father's. I must tell you about Ashok. He is no ordinary businessman: keeping fish is a passion with him. He is far more interested in chatting with his customers about fish than making money selling them. I have never seen him forcing any of his customers to buy from his stock of aquarium fish.

In fact, it was Ashok who introduced me to the amazing world of aquarium fish way back when I was just nine and studying in Class V. Under his guidance then, I experimented with breeding guppies, platties and mollies, fairly simple types of fish to breed. However, it was a matter of great excitement for me at that time to be successful in my experiments and Ashok was generous enough to even buy back from me the baby fish I reared just to encourage me. Later I developed sufficient confidence to experiment with and breed more difficult types of fish, like Siamese Fighting Fish and Blue Guramies—all under the expert tutelage of Ashok.

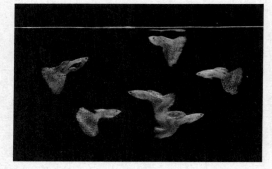

So it was to Ashok's shop that I went every morning at 9.00 a.m., speeding on my bicycle to be on time. I would stay there until lunch time, a regular hands on, doing whatever I was asked to do.

During my first few days at his shop, my work was only to watch the tanks, clean those which were dirty, remove the dead fish and do some other small jobs. I also fed the fish and treated the wounded and diseased fish. Sometimes, I also attended to customers. Gradually, I began to accompany Ashok on his rounds to various places.

I went to clients to fix aquarium equipment such as air pumps and filters, to fix toys in the tanks, to check fish for diseases or if there was a sudden crisis such as fish dying in numbers, or if a client wished to add more fish to his collection. I was sent to collect overdue payments or simply to enquire how the aquariums were doing. Sometimes I went on my own to visit some of the places where we had set up tanks and enjoyed watching the fish swimming happily in their new homes.

During this period I improved my knowledge about aquarium fish tremendously. This was mainly due to two things. Firstly, I had spent a lot of time observing the fish at Ashok's shop and getting practical experience from the places we visited. Secondly, I had been reading the fish books that my father bought for me as a gift for getting a distinction in my SSC exam. The books were quite expensive but well worth the cost. Being able to get theoretical knowledge and practical experience at the same time gave me a lot of confidence with regard to aquarium fish.

Strategies you used for comprehending and reading critically:

_____

_____

Short-Response Questions

1. The author of this excerpt from *Free from School* tells us about how he learned about aquarium fish and about the world of running a small business. Complete the chart below by identifying an example of one way the character in the story learned about aquarium fish and an example of one way he learned about the world of small business.

How the Character Learned About Fish	How the Character Learned About Business

From the sideline: In your answer, be sure you
- *Choose one answer for each column from the passage*
- *Answer the question, "How?"*

Strategies you used: _____

2. Using details from the excerpt from *Free from School*, tell why working in the aquarium shop was an experience that helped the character learn to "manage on [his] own."

> *From the sideline:*
> ■ *What is the question asking? Underline key phrases that focus in on what you should include in your answer.*

_____

_____

_____

_____

> *From the sideline: Be sure your answer*
> ■ *Tells why working in the shops helped the character "manage on [his] own," and*
> ■ *Gives details from the story to support your answer.*

Strategies you used: _____

Hans Christian Andersen is a famous Danish author of children's stories and poems. He was born in Odense, Denmark, in 1805.

EXCERPT FROM *THE TRUE STORY OF MY LIFE*

Hans Christian Andersen

During the last year I had saved together a little sum of money. When I counted it over I found it to be thirteen rix dollars banco (about thirty shillings)[1]. I was quite overjoyed at the possession of so much wealth, and, as my mother now most resolutely required that I should be apprenticed to a tailor, I prayed and besought her that I might make a journey to Copenhagen[2], that I might see the greatest city in the world. "What wilt thou do there?" asked my mother.

"I will become famous," returned I, and I then told her all that I had read about extraordinary men. "People have," said I, "at first an immense deal of adversity to go through, and then they will be famous."

It was a wholly unintelligible impulse that guided me. I wept, I prayed, and at last my mother consented, after having first sent for a so-called wise woman out of the hospital, that she might read my future fortune by the coffee-grounds and cards.

"Your son will become a great man," said the old woman, "and in honor of him, Odense[3] will one day be illuminated."

My mother wept when she heard that, and I obtained permission to travel. All the neighbors told my mother that it was a dreadful thing to let me, at only fourteen years of age, go to Copenhagen, which was such a long way off, and such a great and intricate city, and where I knew nobody.

"Yes," replied my mother, "but he lets me have no peace; I have therefore given my consent, but I am sure that he will go no further than Nyborg[4]; when he gets sight of the rough sea, he will be frightened and turn back again."

The whole day and the following night I travelled through cities and villages; I stood solitarily by the carriage, and ate my bread while [the carriage] was repacked. I thought I was far away in the wide world.

---

[1] A rix dollar banco and shillings are types of coins and money used in the past in European countries.
[2] Copenhagen is a city in Denmark.
[3] Hans Christian Andersen was one of the most famous residents of the city of Odense, Denmark.
[4] Nyborg is another city in Denmark.

Strategies you used for comprehending and reading critically:

_____

_____

Short-Response Questions

3. Why, at fourteen years old, did Hans Christian Andersen want to go to Copenhagen so badly? Use details from the passage to support your answer.

_____

_____

_____

_____

> *From the sideline: Be sure your answer*
> ■ *Explains why Andersen wanted to go to Copenhagen*
> ■ *Uses details from the article to support your response.*

Strategies you used:

_____

_____

4. Why did the mother probably weep at the old woman's reading of the coffee grounds and cards?

_____

_____

_____

_____

Strategies you used:

_____

_____

Extended-Response Question

PLANNING PAGE

Use this page to PLAN your writing for question 5. DO NOT write your final answer here. Anything you write on the planning page will NOT count toward your final score. Write your FINAL answer on the lines that follow the question.

From the sideline: Your planning page could consist of
- *A graphic organizer to illustrate the organization of our essay (see the Online Resources section of this chapter for ideas),*
- *An outline, or*
- *Well-organized notes sequencing several paragraphs and bulleting within each paragraph.*

From the sideline: Check.
- *Does your plan focus on answering the question? Reread the question to be sure. If so, continue. If not, go back and revise to refocus.*
- *Does your plan express your judgment or opinion based on details from the passage?*

5. In both stories, young men are eager to go out and see the world. They both have to learn valuable lessons first. Write an essay in which you describe what you need to do to prepare to go out into the world on your own. Use details from *Free from School* and *The True Story of My Life* to support your description.
   In your response,

   ■ Describe how you would prepare yourself,

   ■ Explain why, and

   ■ Use details from both stories to support your answer.

> *From the sideline: Also, be sure to*
> ■ *Organize your essay into paragraphs (for example: introduction, body, and conclusion) and*
> ■ *Check your writing for correct spelling, punctuation, and grammar.*

_____

_____

_____

_____

_____

_____

_____

_____

_____

_____

_____

_____

_____

_____

_____

_____

> *From the sideline: Check.*
> ▪ *Reread the question to stay focused.*
> ▪ *Are you still focused on answering the question? If so, continue. If not, go back and revise to refocus.*

_____

_____

_____

_____

_____

_____

_____

_____

_____

_____

_____

_____

_____

_____

_____

_____

> *From the sideline: Be sure your essay answers the question. Does it*
> ▪ *Describe how you would prepare yourself,*
> ▪ *Explain why, and*
> ▪ *Use details from both stories to support your answer?*

Strategies you used:

_____

_____

SCORING

Now, let's assess your writing. Typically, Book 3 of the state test looks at

Meaning: Does your answer show you understand the stories and how to answer the questions?

> Have you answered the question completely?

> Does your answer show you understand and can interpret the ideas and the topic or theme of the stories?

> Can you connect the stories to other things you know and other experiences?

Development: Is your answer strong?

> Does your response express your ideas thoroughly and elaborate with details?

> Have you pulled relevant examples from the story to show that you understand?

Organization: Is your writing structured and easy to follow?

> Is your response focused? Do you stick to the point?

> Have you sequenced your ideas so they make sense?

> Have you used transitions between paragraphs and ideas?

Language Use: Is your language interesting and intelligent?

> Have you written in a way that flows easily, engages the reader, and rouses interest?

> Have you used interesting vocabulary, such as vivid adjectives and descriptive adverbs that show a high level of vocabulary knowledge and use?

> Have you varied the way you structure your sentences?

Conventions: How are your grammar, punctuation, and spelling?

> Have you proofread your writing carefully?

> Do you have several paragraphs that provide an overall structure?

Now, go back to your responses and see what you can do to improve them and your writing before you move on to check the possible responses following Appendix C. Which parts do you want to improve on when you take the first practice exam at the end of the book?

ONLINE RESOURCES

Here are some informative websites that will help you prepare for Book 3.

■ To learn more about the writing process, go to *http://www.angelfire.com/wi/writingprocess/prewriting.html*.

■ To learn more about critical reading and writing, visit *http://www.csuohio.edu/academic/writingcenter/critread.html*.

■ To see more examples of graphic organizers, go to *http://www.edhelper.com/teachers/Sorting_graphic_organizers.htm* or *http://www.edhelper.com/teachers/Sequencing_graphic_organizers.htm*.

■ And, to discover more about writing for an audience, check out *http://writing.colostate.edu/guides/processes/audmod/pop2c.cfm*.

CONGRATULATIONS!

Now you know what Book 3 is all about. You have read about the makeup of the test, the test directions, and the question breakdown. You learned three new key points to help you do well. You have also practiced strategies for

■ Reading critically and

■ Planning and writing critical responses

while you practiced sample questions.

Next, take a break. Digest everything you've learned so far. The next time you pick up this book, be prepared to take the first part of the test, Book 1, of Practice Test 1. Review all of the test-taking strategies and tips you've learned so that when you return to start Book 1, you are refreshed and ready to do your best. Remember, you'll need approximately 70 minutes to do Book 1 in full.

By taking this first practice test, you will apply everything you've learned so far. Don't forget to use the strategies suggested in the previous chapters and to review the terminology presented in Appendix A and Appendix B.

APPENDIX

A. LITERARY GENRES

autobiography—The true story of a person's life written by that person.

biography—The true story of a person's life written by someone else.

diary or journal—Dated, personal entries of the writer's feelings, thoughts, and telling of events. We can learn about history by reading journals of people who lived in the past.

fable—A story that teaches a lesson or has a moral. Usually its characters are animals, nonhuman objects, or forces of nature that are given human qualities. *The Tortoise and the Hare* is a popular example of a fable.

fairy tale—A pretend story that features magical, enchanted characters, such as fairies, elves, witches, giants, or talking animals. We usually think of fairy tales as beginning with "Once upon a time . . ." and ending with ". . . and they lived happily ever after." *Shrek* and *Cinderella* are fairy tales.

fantasy—A pretend story that takes place in an imaginary, magical world of its own. This world may have its own rules, language, and culture. *The Lord of the Rings* is an example of a fantasy that takes place in a fantasy world.

folktales—Stories that are passed down orally from generation to generation.

historical fiction—A fictional story that is based on a real event, person, or circumstance in the past. The surroundings of the story may be true, but the story itself did not happen exactly the same way as told. *The Last of the Mohicans* and the American Girl series are examples of historical fiction.

how-to pieces—Writings that give you step-by-step directions on how to complete an activity.

informative pieces—Writings that provide the reader with factual information about a given topic. The writer's opinion is not included.

interviews—A conversation in which one person questions another to elicit thoughts or ideas.

letters—Written correspondence, either friendly or businesslike, from one person to another.

mystery—A story whose plot revolves around finding a solution to a crime or a whodunit situation. Nate the Great and Sherlock Holmes were always solving mysteries.

myth—A story that uses the supernatural to explain natural events. Myths are linked to the spiritual life of a community. There are many myths of Greek gods and goddesses, such as Zeus.

plays—stage representations of stories. Also referred to as drama.

poems—compositions in verse rather than prose. Uses vivid imagery to convey complex emotions, ideas, and experiences.

reports—formal accounts of proceedings, transactions, or events.

science fiction—Called sci-fi, for short, a story that takes place in the future, involves speculations based on current technology and science, and usually goes beyond what can really happen in nature. Stories about time travel and outer space aliens are sci-fi.

tall tale—A humorously exaggerated story that explains a natural phenomenon. For example, the giant footsteps of the lumberjack Paul Bunyan and his blue ox, Babe, formed Minnesota's ten thousand lakes. Bunyan also dug the Grand Canyon by dragging his big ax behind him.

B. GLOSSARY

active listener—Someone who not only hears what is being said but listens for deeper meaning. This type of listener can recall the context of what is said and can analyze it for greater understanding.

analyze—To break something down into parts and see how the parts are related to each other. When we analyze a text, we look at and evaluate its source, its meaning, opposing viewpoints, and so on.

character traits—The qualities that make up a character's personality, including how he or she thinks, acts, feels, and behaves.

context clues—Little suggestions that help readers figure out the meaning of an unfamiliar word by using the meaning of the other words in the sentence or paragraph.

contrast—To find the differences between two or more characters, events, and so on.

essay—A nonfiction piece of writing that focuses on a topic from a limited perspective.

evaluate—To examine or review.

fact—Something that can be proven.

fiction—An imaginary story.

genre—A category of types of writing or reading.

grammatical errors—Errors in sentence organization, word usage, verb tense, and noun/verb relationships.

graphic organizer—A visual representation of how details are related or connected to each other. Examples: a t-chart, a Venn diagram, a timeline.

homonyms—Words that sound the same but are spelled differently and have different meanings.

hyperbole—A great exaggeration.

imagery—Words and phrases that come from the five senses.

interpret—To explain the meaning of something. When we interpret a text, we construct the diverse social, historical, and cultural dimensions it might represent.

main idea—The primary point the author makes in the piece.

metaphor—A comparison of two things that are unlike but may have one thing in common, without using the word *like* or *as* in the comparison. Example: The highway was a winding ribbon.

meter—In poetry, the arrangement of words or lines in a pattern or rhythm that is regularly measured and predictable. A rhythm or beat is felt when the poem is read.

motivation—A character's reason for acting, thinking, or feeling a certain way.

narrative—Any piece that tells a story.

nonfiction—A piece of writing that is true.

onomatopoeia—Using words that sound like what they mean. Examples: hiss, bang, whack.

opinion—Something a person believes to be true but cannot prove as fact.

personification—Giving animals or inanimate objects human characteristics. Example: talking dogs.

plot—Related, sequenced events that make up a story.

point of view—The vantage point from which a story is told. Examples: first person, second person, and third person. First person uses the pronoun *I*, second person uses the pronoun *you*, and third person uses the pronouns *he*, *she*, and *they*.

predict—To guess the ending or the outcome of a series of events or actions.

process of elimination—To remove choices that are obviously incorrect in order to narrow the number of items from which you have to choose.

rubric—An assessment tool used to measure progress or achievement.

run-on sentences—Two or more sentences that are combined as one instead of being separated with the proper punctuation.

sentence fragments—Incomplete sentences that are missing either a noun or a verb.

sequencing—Organizing events in the proper chronological order.

setting—The physical place and time in which a story takes place.

simile—A comparison of two things that are unlike but may have one thing in common, using the word *like* or *as* in the comparison. Example: The highway was like a winding ribbon.

stanza—A grouping of two or more lines in a poem, like a paragraph in an essay.

summarize—To pull together the important ideas in a piece and stating them in your own words.

t-chart—A graphic or visual representation of information that is set in two or more columns with headings for each category. Each column lists a separate viewpoint of a topic.

testing accommodations—Changes made in testing location or method in order to meet the needs of students with special education programs.

theme—An idea that is repeated throughout a piece.

timeline—A graphic or visual representation of events in the chronological order in which they occur.

Venn diagram—A graphic or visual representation of the organization of similarities and differences between two items that are being compared.

verb tense—The past, present, or future form of an action word.

voice—A writer's style of expression.

web—A graphic or visual representation of information displayed with circles and lines that are interconnected in a way to show the relationships between each idea or event.

writing mechanics—A writer's use of capitalization, punctuation, and spelling.

C. ANSWERS TO CHAPTER REVIEW QUESTIONS

CHAPTER 4
Sample Passage A

1. **B** Not only is the tone of the passage one of surprise and amazement as each writer's prediction is discussed, but in the third sentence, the author uses the word *surprisingly* in describing the fact that the writers' ideas did "come to pass."

2. **A** The main idea of the passage is that science fiction writers have made some surprising predictions about the development of technology in the future. The only sentence that supports this main idea is A. While the other three choices are most likely true, they do not directly support the main idea.

3. **D** Answers A, B, and C cannot be assumed based on the details of this passage. Only answer D is supported by the facts in the passage.

Sample Passage B

1. **D** Modern soldiers don't march with drummers, but soldiers in the Civil War did. This quote is a solid clue that the war was not a modern war. The other three choices are not supported by this quote or by the rest of the passage.

2. **A** Jo acts the most impatient when she tells everyone to hurry. She even chokes on her tea and drops her bread. The other girls act more calmly and patiently. Beth sits in the corner and waits.

3. **C** Jo is telling Amy not to worry about eating politely because she doesn't want to wait any longer than she has to in order to hear Father's letter.

Sample Passage C

1. **B** Although other readers might enjoy this passage, it is largely about having a ferret as a pet. Therefore, someone thinking of adopting a ferret would be **most** interested because it contains a good deal of specific information about ferrets as pets.

2. **A** The fact that, historically, ferrets were used for hunting, protection, and companionship shows they are useful and trainable animals.

3. **C** Ferrets and polecats are both from the Mustelidae family. Animals in this family all have scent glands under their tails. The rest of the choices are mentioned but are not said to be true of both the polecat and the ferret.

CHAPTER 5

Multiple-Choice Questions

1. **B** All of the choices were mentioned at various points in the listening passage. In this question, however, the key phrases to focus on are "when he was a child" and "physical trait." Stamina and determination are two personality traits that Terry exhibited. They are not physical traits. The artificial leg is a physical trait, but Terry did not have it as a child. Therefore, his height is the only appropriate choice.

2. **D** The key word in this question is *except*. All of the choices are things that Terry Fox specifically set as goals for himself, except for becoming a national hero. This happened as a result of his other goals.

3. **A** The key phrase in this question is "best be described." Although there may have been points in his life when he felt anxious, negative, or content, *unwavering* is the adjective that can be used consistently to describe Terry. *Unwavering* is a synonym for *determined*, an adjective that is used repeatedly to describe Terry Fox. It can also be used alongside *stamina* and *endurance*, which are other adjectives that are used to describe him throughout the passage.

4. **C** Although the article may be entertaining for some, it is considered a biography because it provides details and information about Terry Fox's life. The article does not attempt to persuade the reader, nor does it make a comparison.

5. **D** The Terry Fox Monument is a proper noun because it is the name of a specific monument in Canada.

6. **A** Sentences B and D are run-on sentences. Sentence C uses a semicolon after the transition *however* when it actually needs a comma.

7. **C** *Wasn't* is a combination of the words *was* and *not*, and the apostrophe is placed where the letter *o* is missing.

8. **D** Commas need to be placed between the sports because it is a list of three or more items. Capital letters are not needed because the words are not proper nouns. The addition of periods would create sentence fragments, and changing the period at the end of the sentence to an exclamation point is unnecessary because the sentence is not a statement that should be filled with excitement.

Short-Response Questions

9. The graphic organizer should be completed similar to the following:

Obstacles or Challenges Terry Faced	How Terry Overcame the Obstacles or Challenges
Wanted to play guard on basketball team, but wasn't a good player	Practiced every day until he made the team; became one of the best guards
Had his leg amputated at age 18 due to cancer	Learned how to use his artificial leg and started running
Wanted to raise $1 from every Canadian for cancer research	Created Marathon of Hope and ran 143 days straight

Another possible answer:

Loved many sports, but he was not very tall—Worked twice as hard as the bigger kids

10. The short response to this question should be similar to the following, including details taken directly from the passage that support the idea that Terry Fox wanted to help others facing cancer, and that he was determined not to let his own disability or illness stand in the way:

Terry Fox showed that he was committed to helping others when he started the Marathon of Hope to raise money for cancer research. Although he had his leg amputated because of cancer, he was determined to run across Canada, from the Atlantic Ocean to the Pacific Ocean, and raise $1 from every Canadian citizen. He showed determination when he learned how to run on his artificial leg in order to achieve his goal. He ran a total of 3,339 miles before his cancer spread to his lungs and he had to stop running. Even though he did not complete his marathon, he showed the world that you can do wonderful things when you are determined and don't give up.

11. Your answer should be similar to the paragraph below:

Although Terry Fox has passed away, the reader can infer that he inspired others to follow his lead. Soon after Terry Fox died, a nationwide telethon was organized in Canada to raise funds for cancer research. By February of 1981, over 24 million dollars had been raised for this cause. Even today, all across Canada, the United States, and other countries, Terry Fox races are organized to raise money for cancer research.

Another possible detail to include in the answer is that the Terry Fox Monument still stands in Thunder Bay, Canada, as a reminder of where his Marathon of Hope ended.

CHAPTER 6

Short-Response Questions

1. The graphic organizer should be completed using details from the passage. Following is a possible answer:

How the Character Learned About Fish	How the Character Learned About Business
The character learned about fish by reading the books about fish that came from the character's father.	The character learned about business by observing how Ashok managed his customers and business.

2. Following is a possible response:

The character's parents wanted him to learn to "manage on [his] own" before he traveled to see the world, so he worked as an apprentice in the aquarium shop. This experience helped him learn skills like how to breed fish and how to manage a small business. He worked with customers and collected payments. He learned what it takes to earn money and to be responsible by doing what Ashok told him to do. The things he learned were skills that would help him gain experience and learn how to manage money.

3. Following is a possible response:

Hans Christian Andersen had a little money in his pocket and wanted to see Copenhagen. He may have also wanted to avoid his mother's idea of him becoming an apprentice tailor. Instead, he said, he wanted to become famous. He said it was an impulse.

4. Following is a possible response:

The mother probably wept because she was so worried about her son. He was very young to be traveling so far by himself, as the neighbors said. She may also have wept because the old woman said that Hans would become famous one day and make the town proud. This may have caused her to weep tears of pride for her son's accomplishments.

Extended-Response Question

5. Possible planning page:

Graphic style:

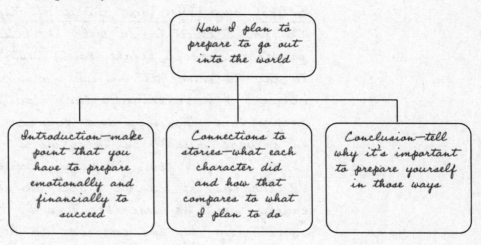

Outline style:

  I. Introduction

  A. Importance of preparing yourself to go out into the world

  B. Prepare emotionally and financially

 II. Connections to stories

  A. How to prepare emotionally

  B. How to prepare financially

III. Conclusion

  A. Why it's important to prepare

Now you are ready to look at an example of how this planning can help you create a solid, organized essay. The following is a possible response:

The characters in the two stories, Free from School and The True Story of My Life, make the point that to do well in life, you should prepare yourself before going out into the world to try to make it on your own. From these stories, I have learned that you have to be prepared emotionally and financially. I plan to prepare myself in these ways.

To begin, I plan to prepare myself emotionally. At the end of Hans's story, he seems very lonely when he describes how he eats his bread "solitarily" by the carriage as he reflects about being so far away from home. He was so young when he left, only fourteen. He didn't seem to do too much thinking or planning before he moved. He said he did it on impulse. To prepare myself emotionally, I will keep close ties with my family. My parents and I are very close now. We talk a lot about what's going on. I don't tell them everything, but it makes me feel good to know they are there when I need them. I want to keep the lines of communication open with them no matter where I am. Cell phones and computers make that easier today than it was back in the days of Hans Christian Andersen and the character in Free from School. (We aren't told his name or if this is an autobiography.)

Furthermore, I plan to prepare financially. It seems that Hans just had a pocketful of money. That won't take him far. He wasn't heading to Copenhagen for any specific job, so he was really taking a big financial risk. The other character was working at the aquarium store to earn money and experience before he moved out. He was smart. I plan to have a hefty savings account and a good job before I move out on my own. I have to be able to afford rent, food, a car payment, and other expenses. I also plan to go to college first so I can have a better chance at getting a good-paying job before I move out.

These two stories made me think a lot about what it takes to move out on my own. It's an exciting thing to think about, but it's really important to be prepared before you make the leap if you want to succeed.

PRACTICE TEST 1

TIPS TO DO YOUR BEST

- Carefully read all the directions.
- Plan how you will use your time wisely.
- Read each question thoroughly.
- Before choosing your response, think about the answer.

BOOK 1: READING

41 Multiple-Choice Questions

70 Minutes to Complete—Work Until You Come to Book 2.

DIRECTIONS

In Book 1, you will read eight or more passages and answer several questions about each one. Fill in the answers to the multiple-choice questions on the bubble sheet on the next page. You may make notes or marks on the test pages as you read. Be sure to answer all of the questions. The correct answers, with explanations, follow this test on pages 170–173.

ANSWER SHEET

Short-response questions in Book 2 and all questions in Book 3 should be answered directly on the test pages.

BOOK 1

1. Ⓐ Ⓑ Ⓒ Ⓓ   15. Ⓐ Ⓑ Ⓒ Ⓓ   29. Ⓐ Ⓑ Ⓒ Ⓓ
2. Ⓐ Ⓑ Ⓒ Ⓓ   16. Ⓐ Ⓑ Ⓒ Ⓓ   30. Ⓐ Ⓑ Ⓒ Ⓓ
3. Ⓐ Ⓑ Ⓒ Ⓓ   17. Ⓐ Ⓑ Ⓒ Ⓓ   31. Ⓐ Ⓑ Ⓒ Ⓓ
4. Ⓐ Ⓑ Ⓒ Ⓓ   18. Ⓐ Ⓑ Ⓒ Ⓓ   32. Ⓐ Ⓑ Ⓒ Ⓓ
5. Ⓐ Ⓑ Ⓒ Ⓓ   19. Ⓐ Ⓑ Ⓒ Ⓓ   33. Ⓐ Ⓑ Ⓒ Ⓓ
6. Ⓐ Ⓑ Ⓒ Ⓓ   20. Ⓐ Ⓑ Ⓒ Ⓓ   34. Ⓐ Ⓑ Ⓒ Ⓓ
7. Ⓐ Ⓑ Ⓒ Ⓓ   21. Ⓐ Ⓑ Ⓒ Ⓓ   35. Ⓐ Ⓑ Ⓒ Ⓓ
8. Ⓐ Ⓑ Ⓒ Ⓓ   22. Ⓐ Ⓑ Ⓒ Ⓓ   36. Ⓐ Ⓑ Ⓒ Ⓓ
9. Ⓐ Ⓑ Ⓒ Ⓓ   23. Ⓐ Ⓑ Ⓒ Ⓓ   37. Ⓐ Ⓑ Ⓒ Ⓓ
10. Ⓐ Ⓑ Ⓒ Ⓓ   24. Ⓐ Ⓑ Ⓒ Ⓓ   38. Ⓐ Ⓑ Ⓒ Ⓓ
11. Ⓐ Ⓑ Ⓒ Ⓓ   25. Ⓐ Ⓑ Ⓒ Ⓓ   39. Ⓐ Ⓑ Ⓒ Ⓓ
12. Ⓐ Ⓑ Ⓒ Ⓓ   26. Ⓐ Ⓑ Ⓒ Ⓓ   40. Ⓐ Ⓑ Ⓒ Ⓓ
13. Ⓐ Ⓑ Ⓒ Ⓓ   27. Ⓐ Ⓑ Ⓒ Ⓓ   41. Ⓐ Ⓑ Ⓒ Ⓓ
14. Ⓐ Ⓑ Ⓒ Ⓓ   28. Ⓐ Ⓑ Ⓒ Ⓓ

BOOK 2

1. Ⓐ Ⓑ Ⓒ Ⓓ   4. Ⓐ Ⓑ Ⓒ Ⓓ   7. Ⓐ Ⓑ Ⓒ Ⓓ
2. Ⓐ Ⓑ Ⓒ Ⓓ   5. Ⓐ Ⓑ Ⓒ Ⓓ   8. Ⓐ Ⓑ Ⓒ Ⓓ
3. Ⓐ Ⓑ Ⓒ Ⓓ   6. Ⓐ Ⓑ Ⓒ Ⓓ

Directions: Read the following article about Mark Twain. Then answer questions 1 through 4.

WAS MARK TWAIN A NATURALIST[1]?

Linda Pratt and J. Michael Pratt

Have you read *The Adventures of Tom Sawyer*, *The Adventures of Huckleberry Finn*, or *The Prince and the Pauper*? What famous American author wrote these books? If your answer was Mark Twain, you were right. If you answered Samuel Clemens, you were also right. "Mark Twain" was the pen name that Clemens used.

Mark Twain's books reflect his travels in America and around the world. In his second book, *Roughing It*, he tells about going out West in 1861 in search of a fortune in gold and silver. Although he never found a fortune, he did have many exciting, memorable adventures exploring and studying the natural world he found in America's Wild West. Was Mark Twain a naturalist?

Twain saw many kinds of wild animals while roaming about America's Far West. Coyotes, prairie dogs, large hairy spiders called tarantulas, and poisonous scorpions were some of them. Many kinds of plants, including sagebrush, colorful flowers, and giant trees also roused his curiosity. Mountains, valleys, lakes, deserts, forests, and islands were some of the wild places that he liked to explore and contemplate[2]. He climbed mountains and even volcanoes to view gorgeous landscapes. Sunsets, clouds in a blue sky, or a gentle breeze often caused Twain to marvel at Nature's spectacular world.

Lake Tahoe was and is famous for its incredibly beautiful scenery. Twain and a few friends hiked from Virginia City in Nevada to see the lake for themselves. After a long, difficult trek, Lake Tahoe finally came into view. They were amazed by what they saw. Spread out before them was a large, oval lake as blue as the sky. High, snow-capped mountains and dense forests surrounded it. While camping out at the lakeshore, Twain and his buddies rowed a small boat across the deep, crystal-clear lake, watched gorgeous sunsets, and even accidentally started a forest fire.

---

[1] **naturalist**—someone who studies the natural world to learn more about it

[2] **contemplate**—to attend to thoughtfully

On a later trip from Virginia City to Carson City, Nevada, he and two friends got lost in a blinding blizzard. When night came, they tried to light a campfire by first firing a pistol into a pile of twigs, then rubbing two sticks together, and finally using matches. No matter what they did, a fire wouldn't start. Tired, cold, and hungry, they bid farewell to each other and lay down in the snow, waiting to freeze to death. However, in the morning everyone awoke, poked their heads out from a pile of new snow, and discovered that they had fallen asleep not more than fifteen steps from a warm stagecoach station. They were all happy to be alive but angry about having slept in the snow all night, believing they would die.

When searching for a hidden gold mine, Twain and a few friends came across Mono Lake. It is a very unusual, odd-looking lake located in a desert high in the Sierra Nevada Mountains of California. He thought the lake was unusual for several reasons. First, he noted that the depth of the lake remained constant even though mountain streams brought water to the lake but none carried any water away. He also observed the water felt soapy, which meant the lake was high in alkali[3]. Furthermore, billions of tiny brine shrimp lived in the lake, making it look gray, and countless flies covered the entire lakeshore, eating dead shrimp. Twain studiously observed the natural features of the lake.

Twain also had sailed to and explored the Hawaiian Islands. These islands formed long ago from volcanoes. After climbing one of the larger volcanoes, he cautiously walked across the main crater[4] at night. What he saw close-up was very hot molten lava leaping high into the air again and again. It fell into a large pool of bubbling lava. He watched as a lava pool overflowed down the side of the volcano. Eventually, the lava reached the sea, where it cooled into solid rock, making the island a bit larger.

Nature and its many wonders fascinated Mark Twain. In *Roughing It*, he tells us much about the natural world he found in America's Wild West and Hawaii. Was Mark Twain a naturalist?

---

[3] **alkali**—a salty chemical compound

[4] **crater**—the opening or basin of a volcano

1. According to the passage, Mark Twain was Samuel Clemens's pen name. This means that
   A. Mark Twain was the name the author was given at birth
   B. Samuel Clemens identified himself as Mark Twain all of the time
   C. Samuel Clemens was a false name
   D. the name Mark Twain appeared as the author on the books Samuel Clemens wrote

2. Which of these sentences from the passage **best** supports the fact that Twain was a naturalist?
   A. "Although he never found a fortune, he did have many exciting, memorable adventures exploring and studying the natural world he found in America's Wild West."
   B. "Twain saw many kinds of wild animals while roaming about America's Far West."
   C. "They were all happy to be alive but angry about having slept in the snow all night, believing they would die."
   D. "When searching for a hidden gold mine, Twain and a few friends came across Mono Lake."

3. This passage would be **most** informative to readers seeking to learn more about
   A. becoming an author
   B. traveling through the Wild West
   C. Mark Twain's adventures and what inspired his writing
   D. American naturalists

4. Which sentence from the passage **best** supports the idea that Twain's adventures inspired his writing?
   A. "Nature and its many wonders fascinated Mark Twain."
   B. "Lake Tahoe was and is famous for its incredibly beautiful scenery."
   C. "Mark Twain's books reflect his travels in America and around the world."
   D. "Many kinds of plants, including sagebrush, colorful flowers, and giant trees also roused his curiosity."

Directions: Read this poem by Robert Lee Frost. Then answer questions 5 through 7.

A MINOR BIRD

Robert Lee Frost

I have wished a bird would fly away,
And not sing by my house all day;

Have clapped my hands at him from the door
When it seemed as if I could bear no more.

The fault must partly have been in me.
The bird was not to blame for his key.

And of course there must be something wrong
In wanting to silence any song.

5. This poem is told from the point of view of

   A. a bird

   B. someone thinking about birds he or she has seen in the past

   C. someone watching a bird

   D. someone hunting a bird

6. Read this stanza from the poem:

   The fault must partly have been in me.
   The bird was not to blame for his key.

   In this stanza, the author most likely means he

   A. realizes his intolerance stopped him from appreciating the bird's song

   B. was wrong to have chased the bird away

   C. was partly the reason the bird couldn't sing well

   D. injured the bird in trying to silence it

7. Which lines from the poem indicate the author may be talking about more than singing birds?

   A. I have wished a bird would fly away,
   And not sing by my house all day;

   B. Have clapped my hands at him from the door
   When it seemed as if I could bear no more.

   C. The fault must partly have been in me.
   The bird was not to blame for his key.

   D. And of course there must be something wrong
   In wanting to silence any song.

Directions: Read this excerpt from *How the Leopard Got His Spots* by Rudyard Kipling. Then answer questions 8 through 14.

EXCERPT FROM "HOW THE LEOPARD GOT HIS SPOTS"

Rudyard Kipling

In this excerpt, the Ethiopian teaches Leopard how to camouflage herself so she can improve her hunting.

"Hi! Hi!" said the Ethiopian. "That's a trick worth learning. Take a lesson by it, Leopard. You show up in this dark place like a bar of soap in a coal-scuttle."

"Ho! Ho!" said the Leopard. "Would it surprise you very much to know that you show up in this dark place like a mustard-plaster on a sack of coals?"

"Well, calling names won't catch dinner," said the Ethiopian. "The long and the little of it is that we don't match our backgrounds. I'm going to take Baviaan's advice. He told me I ought to change. And, as I've nothing to change except my skin, I'm going to change that."

"What to?" said the Leopard, tremendously excited.

"To a nice working blackish-brownish color, with a little purple in it, and touches of slaty-blue. It will be the very thing for hiding in hollows and behind trees."

So he changed his skin then and there, and the Leopard was more excited than ever. He had never seen a man change his skin before.

"But what about me?" she said when the Ethiopian had worked his last little finger into his fine new black skin.

"You take Baviaan's advice, too. He told you to go into spots . . . . He meant spots on your skin."

"What's the use of that?" said the Leopard.

"Think of Giraffe," said the Ethiopian. "Or, if you prefer stripes, think of Zebra. They find their spots and stripes give them perfect satisfaction."

"Umm," said the Leopard. "I wouldn't look like Zebra—not for ever so."

"Well, make up your mind," said the Ethiopian, "because I'd hate to go hunting without you. But, I must if you insist on looking like a sunflower against a tarred fence."

"I'll take spots, then," said the Leopard. "But, don't make 'em too vulgar-big. I wouldn't look like Giraffe—not for ever so."

"I'll make 'em with the tips of my fingers," said the Ethiopian. "There's plenty of black left on my skin still. Stand over!"

Then the Ethiopian put his five fingers close together (there was plenty of black left on his new skin still) and pressed them all over the Leopard. Wherever the five fingers touched, they left five little black marks, all close together. You can see them on any Leopard's skin you like, Best Beloved. Sometimes the fingers slipped and the marks got a little blurred; but if you look closely at any Leopard now, you will see that there are always five spots—off five black finger-tips.

8. Read these sentences from the excerpt:

   You show up in this dark place like a bar of soap in a coal-scuttle. Would it surprise you very much to know that you show up in this dark place like a mustard-plaster on a sack of coals? But, I must if you insist on looking like a sunflower against a tarred fence.

   Which literary device does the author use in these sentences?

   A. simile

   B. personification

   C. hyperbole

   D. flashback

9. This excerpt could be used to explain

   A. how to survive in dark places

   B. why leopards have spots

   C. how to be an expert hunter

   D. how to trap zebras and giraffes

10. Read this sentence from the excerpt:

    You can see them on any Leopard's skin you like, Best Beloved.

    In this sentence, "Best Beloved" is most likely

    A. Leopard

    B. the Ethiopian

    C. the author

    D. the person with whom the storyteller is sharing this story

11. According to the excerpt, Baviaan is

    A. the Ethiopian's friend

    B. Leopard's brother

    C. the ruler of the kingdom

    D. The excerpt does not explain who Baviaan is.

12. When the Ethiopian refers to matching the "background," he is most likely talking about the Leopard and him

    A. blending in with the environment so their prey won't see them

    B. coordinating their furniture so it will match

    C. doing what their families would have done in the same situation

    D. waiting until the seasons change so the background colors match

13. Which sentence from the excerpt **best** supports the fact that the Ethiopian and the Leopard are hunting companions and possibly good friends?

    A. "Well, calling names won't catch dinner," said the Ethiopian.

    B. "Well, make up your mind," said the Ethiopian, "because I'd hate to go hunting without you."

    C. "I'll make 'em with the tips of my fingers," said the Ethiopian.

    D. Then the Ethiopian put his five fingers close together (there was plenty of black left on his new skin still) and pressed them all over the Leopard.

14. Where does this conversation between the Ethiopian and the Leopard **most likely** take place?

    A. in the Arctic

    B. in the desert

    C. at a zoo

    D. in a jungle

Directions: Read this passage about elephants. Then answer questions 15 through 20.

THEN THERE WERE THREE . . . AN ELEPHANT TALE

Carolyn F. Chryst

A million years ago, giant elephant-like beasts with shaggy hair and huge, curved tusks wandered the Great Plains of North America. The *Mammuthus*—or mammoths—were close relatives to modern elephants. Elephants and mammoths both belong to the scientific order Proboscidea and to the family Elephantidae. Scientists believe that over 350 different kinds of Proboscidea have roamed the earth. Today, however, there are only three types of Proboscidea remaining: Asian, African Bush, and African Forest elephants.

The Asian elephant, *Elephas maximus*, is a senior member of the Elephantidae family. The Asian elephant's family tree goes further back in time than the African elephant's or the mammoth's. Some scientists believe that the age of the Asian elephant's family tree may help explain why they are more coordinated than their "younger" cousins, the African elephants. The Asian elephant has had more time to develop efficient adaptations to its environment. Scientists also suggest that Asian elephants and extinct mammoths are more closely related to each other than either one is to the African elephants. The Asian elephant and the mammoth have many similar physical characteristics, such as small ears and a complex rectangular tooth ridge pattern. Furthermore, their tallest point is measured from their heads.

The younger African elephant family tree has two types of elephants. Scientists recently discovered that the DNA differences between African bush and African forest elephants were as big as the difference between African and

African bush elephant

African forest elephant

Asian elephants. The African elephant has large fan-like ears and a simple diamond-pattern tooth ridge. Also, its back is concave like a horse's back, as shown in the side-angled picture of the African forest elephant.

A critical difference between the extinct mammoth and all modern elephants is the size and weight of the tusks. A mammoth's tusk could grow to 16 feet and weigh well over 200 pounds. The modern male elephant's tusk rarely reaches 10 feet and weighs between 13 and 21 pounds. Many scientists believe that the mammoth's long, heavy tusks may have contributed to its extinction.

An inability to adapt to changes in environment may have contributed to the loss of the other 349 Proboscidea. Unfortunately, all three modern elephants currently face extinction. Their biggest threat to survival is humans.

15. Read this sentence from the passage:

Some scientists believe that the age of the Asian elephant's family tree may help explain why they are more coordinated than their "younger" cousins, the African elephants.

Why did the author put quotation marks around the word *younger*?

A. The marks emphasize that the Asian and African elephants are related.

B. Scientists typically use quotation marks to highlight relevant ages.

C. When you are talking about millions of years, the term *younger* is relative, or less significant.

D. We don't really know if they are younger or not.

16. Which sentence from the passage supports the idea that scientists have traced Asian elephants back further than the mammoths?

    A. Scientists recently discovered that the DNA differences between African bush and African forest elephants were as big as the difference between African and Asian elephants.

    B. The *Mammuthus*—or mammoths—were close relatives to modern elephants.

    C. The Asian elephant's family tree goes further back in time than the African elephant's or the mammoth's.

    D. The Asian elephant has had more time to develop efficient adaptations to its environment.

17. The mood the author creates at the end of the passage is **best** described as

    A. gloom

    B. carefree

    C. suspense

    D. excitement

18. According to the passage, it is likely that the mammoth became extinct because

    A. people hunted them for their tusks

    B. their tusks restricted them from running away from their prey

    C. their tusks were too heavy for them to support over time

    D. We are not told why the tusks may have contributed to the mammoth's extinction.

19. One similarity between the Asian elephant and the mammoth is that

    A. their tusks weigh or weighed approximately 200 pounds

    B. their backs are convex

    C. they have the same DNA

    D. their tallest point is measured from their heads

20. To what does the title of this passage, "Then There Were Three . . . An Elephant Tale," refer?

    A. There are only three types of Proboscidea remaining on Earth.

    B. What would happen if there were only three elephants left on Earth?

    C. There are three distinct differences between the Asian and African elephants.

    D. There are three types of mammoths remaining on Earth.

Directions: Read this passage. Then answer questions 21 through 28.

COMPUTERS IN OUR LIVES

Akshar Shastri

Today, computers have transformed everyday life in dramatic ways. However, this Computer Age, sometimes called the Information Age, has been a relatively recent development. Computers have made access to knowledge and information fast and easy. As people become more familiar with the computer, it has become increasingly useful to the human population and prevalent in society.

Initially, people could not use computers easily due to the complex operating systems[1]. As a result, only sophisticated, professional computer users could use computers. For this trend to change, the operating system on the computers had to be modified so novices could quickly and easily use them. A company by the name of Microsoft saw this opportunity in the market and quickly capitalized upon it.

Before the 1980s, computers were a mere luxury. Only wealthy people could afford them. Additionally, computer systems were big and bulky and, therefore, could not fit easily into one's home. However, with the invention of a tiny electronic circuit known as a silicon chip that can hold billions of bits of information, computers became compact, practical, and a part of everyday life. Furthermore, in 1985, as the chief executive officer of Microsoft, Bill Gates developed Microsoft Windows, which revolutionized personal computers by making them user-friendly to amateur users.

---

[1] **operating system**—the technology that allows the user to access the information the computer holds

The popularity of computers, including the personal computer, or PC, is due to the unlimited capabilities and applications for them. Computers can process information with astonishing speed and accuracy. Whether you are writing a report or shopping for a car, helpful information from around the world can be at your fingertips within moments. All you need to do is search online for a particular topic, and a list of relevant websites from which you can choose will pop up on the screen. Computers come in all shapes and sizes, and sometimes you may not even realize a computer exists in close proximity. Just because a laptop is not sitting on a table in a room, it does not mean there are no computers in the room. For example, an electronic thermostat may be in the room, constantly sensing the temperature and operating a furnace when needed. An electronic thermostat makes a furnace more efficient because the user can program it. It can be turned off during the afternoon when no one is home or at night when everyone is cozy under their bed covers. Then, when one returns home from work or wakes up, the house can be warm if the furnace comes on shortly before one needs to use the house. Thanks to the small computer inside the thermostat, a family could save hundreds of dollars on the heating bill and remain comfortable.

Computers have come a long way. The tasks that computers can do today were previously impossible or were inefficient. On a daily basis, people use computers to advance in the workplace and to simply relax at home. What future computer advancements will develop? How will human lives be affected? The possibilities are limited only by our imagination.

21. Based on the information in the passage, readers can conclude that the author

A. owns a PC

B. supports the use of computers in schools

C. believes computers are helpful to people

D. believes computers are a luxury

22. This passage would be **most** informative to a reader who is writing a report about

A. different types of computers

B. Bill Gates

C. how computers have transformed our everyday lives

D. Microsoft Windows

23. According to the passage, the Computer Age

    A. began in 1985
    B. is sometimes referred to as the Information Age
    C. was sparked by the silicon chip
    D. will never end

24. Look at the sample index below.

    Gates, "Bill" William Henry
        childhood, 67
        Foundation, 65
        Microsoft, 68
        wealth, 70

    On which page would you be most likely to find the answer to this question: How did Bill Gates come up with the idea for the Windows operating system?

    A. 65
    B. 67
    C. 68
    D. 70

25. According to the author, an electronic thermostat is a computer because

    A. it can be programmed
    B. it produces heat
    C. people can save money by turning it off
    D. it is user-friendly

26. Read this sentence from the passage:

    Furthermore, in 1985, as the chief executive officer of Microsoft, Bill Gates developed Microsoft Windows, which revolutionized personal computers by making them user-friendly to amateur users.

    In this sentence, the author implies that

    A. amateur users are less knowledgeable about using computers than professional users are

    B. amateur users are generally less intelligent than professional users are

    C. Bill Gates is an amateur user

    D. amateur users still currently prefer using Microsoft Windows over any other operating system

27. One detail from the passage that shows that computers can save us time is

    A. information can be found online and at your fingertips in a moment

    B. computers now come in all shapes and sizes

    C. you can program your thermostat to make your furnace efficient

    D. people use computers in the workplace and at home

28. According to the passage, computers are more user friendly for all of the following reasons except

    A. they are small, portable, and can fit into the average home

    B. the operating system is easy enough for amateurs to use

    C. in the 1980s computers were owned only by the wealthy

    D. information can be found on the Internet with astonishing speed

Directions: Read this poem. Then answer questions 29 through 33.

WORDS

Ella Wheeler Wilcox

Words are great forces in the realm of life;
    Be careful of their use. Who talks of hate,
Of poverty, or sickness, but sets rife
    These very elements to mar his fate.

When love, health, happiness, and plenty hear
    Their names repeated over day by day,
They wing their way like answering fairies near,
    Then nestle down within our homes to stay.

Who talks of evil conjures into shape
    The formless thing and gives it life and scope.
This is the law: then let no word escape
    That does not breathe of everlasting hope.

29. This poem uses all of the following except

    A. free verse

    B. rhyme schemes

    C. imagery

    D. stanzas

30. Read the following lines from the poem:

    When love, health, happiness, and plenty hear
        Their names repeated over day by day,
    They wing their way like answering fairies near.

    The lines above include what two types of figurative language?

    A. hyperbole and metaphor

    B. personification and simile

    C. onomatopoeia and irony

    D. alliteration and rhyme

31. Which word below describes the way the *words* in the poem are characterized?

    A. vague

    B. apprehensive

    C. confident

    D. influential

32. Read the following line from the poem:

    Words are great forces in the realm of life

    The word *realm* means the same as

    A. health

    B. family

    C. space

    D. emotions

33. The tone of this poem is one of

    A. caution

    B. anger

    C. distress

    D. grief

Directions: Read this fable. Then answer questions 34 through 38.

THE FOX AND THE GOAT

A Fox one day fell into a deep well and could find no means of escape. A Goat, overcome with thirst, came to the same well, and seeing the Fox, inquired if the water was good. Concealing his sad plight under a merry guise, the Fox indulged in a lavish praise of the water, saying it was excellent beyond measure, and encouraging him to descend. The Goat, mindful only of his thirst, thoughtlessly jumped down, but just as he drank, the Fox informed him of the difficulty they were both in and suggested a scheme for their common escape.

"If," said he, "you will place your forefeet upon the wall and bend your head, I will run up your back and escape, and will help you out afterwards."

The Goat readily assented and the Fox leaped upon his back. Steadying himself with the Goat's horns, he safely reached the mouth of the well and made off as fast as he could.

When the Goat upbraided him for breaking his promise, he turned around and cried out, "You foolish old fellow! If you had as many brains in your head as you have hairs in your beard, you would never have gone down before you had inspected the way up, nor have exposed yourself to dangers from which you had no means of escape."

34. Read the following sentence from the fable:

> **Concealing his sad plight under a merry guise, the Fox indulged in a lavish praise of the water.**

Based on this sentence, a synonym for the word *concealing* is

A. displaying

B. uncovering

C. smiling

D. hiding

35. What character trait can best describe the Goat?

    A. intelligent

    B. gullible

    C. furious

    D. careless

36. Read the following sentence from the fable:

    The Goat upbraided him for breaking his promise.

    Based on the context of the story, what does the word *upbraided* mean?

    A. scolded

    B. praised

    C. thanked

    D. questioned

37. **Most likely,** the Goat joined the Fox in the well because

    A. he did not want him to die in the well

    B. he wanted to become his friend

    C. he was thirsty and wanted the water

    D. he trusted that the Fox was truthful

38. What is **most likely** the moral of this fable?

    A. Look before you leap.

    B. Never judge a book by its cover.

    C. Better to give than to receive.

    D. Never trust a wolf in sheep's clothing.

Directions: Read the following excerpt from the autobiography of Helen Keller, who became both deaf and blind after falling ill when she was two years old. This passage describes when Helen's teacher, Annie Sullivan, finally makes a breakthrough with her. After you have finished reading, answer questions 39 through 41.

The morning after my teacher came she led me into her room and gave me a doll. The little blind children at the Perkins Institution had sent it and Laura Bridgman had dressed it; but I did not know this until afterward. When I had played with it a little while, Miss Sullivan slowly spelled into my hand the word "d-o-l-l." I was at once interested in this finger play and tried to imitate it. When I finally succeeded in making the letters correctly I was flushed with childish pleasure and pride. Running downstairs to my mother I held up my hand and made the letters for doll. I did not know that I was spelling a word or even that words existed; I was simply making my fingers go in monkey-like imitation. In the days that followed I learned to spell in this uncomprehending way a great many words, among them pin, hat, cup and a few verbs like sit, stand and walk. But my teacher had been with me several weeks before I understood that everything has a name.

One day, while I was playing with my new doll, Miss Sullivan put my big rag doll into my lap also, spelled "d-o-l-l," and tried to make me understand that "d-o-l-l" applied to both. Earlier in the day we had had a tussle over the words "m-u-g" and "w-a-t-e-r." Miss Sullivan had tried to impress it upon me that "m-u-g" is mug and that "w-a-t-e-r" is water, but I persisted in confounding the two. In despair she had dropped the subject for the time, only to renew it at the first opportunity. I became impatient at her repeated attempts and, seizing the new doll, I dashed it upon the floor. I was keenly delighted when I felt the fragments of the broken doll at my feet. Neither sorrow nor regret followed my passionate outburst. I had not loved the doll. In the still, dark world in which I lived there was no strong sentiment or tenderness. I felt my teacher sweep the fragments to one side of the hearth, and I had a sense of satisfaction that the cause of my discomfort was removed. She brought me my hat, and I knew I was going out into the warm sunshine. This thought, if a wordless sensation may be called a thought, made me hop and skip with pleasure.

We walked down the path to the well-house, attracted by the fragrance of the honeysuckle with which it was covered. Someone was drawing water and my teacher placed my hand under the spout. As the cool stream gushed over one hand she spelled into the other the word water, first slowly, then rapidly. I stood still, my whole attention fixed upon the motions of her fingers. Suddenly I felt a misty consciousness as of something forgotten—a thrill of returning thought; and somehow the mystery of language was revealed to me. I knew then that "w-a-t-e-r" meant the wonderful cool something that was flowing over my hand. That living word awakened my soul, gave it light, hope, joy, set it free! There were barriers still, it is true, but barriers that could in time be swept away.

39. When Miss Sullivan first spells the word "doll" onto Helen's palm, the reader can infer that Helen thinks

  A. the hand movements represent letters

  B. Miss Sullivan is giving her doll a name

  C. her teacher is trying to play a game

  D. her teacher is teaching her how to spell

40. When Miss Sullivan keeps spelling the word "water" onto Helen's hand over and over again, this demonstrates that Miss Sullivan is

  A. determined

  B. impatient

  C. aggravated

  D. ruthless

41. What lesson or lessons can the reader learn from Miss Sullivan and Helen's experience?

  A. If at first you don't succeed, try again.

  B. No obstacle is too great to overcome.

  C. Everyone can learn if they are willing to try.

  D. All of the above.

BOOK 2: LISTENING AND WRITING MECHANICS

8 Multiple-Choice Questions
3 Short-Response Questions
30 Minutes to Complete—Work Until You Come to Book 3.

> *Note to Reader:* Remove the story from the rest of the test, leaving the note pages for the student to take notes on while you read the directions and passage twice.

Directions: You will hear a passage called "Children's Books Triumph Over Tragedy" by Alison Black. You will listen to the passage two times. You may take notes at any time as you listen to the passage. Then you will use your notes to help you answer the questions that follow. Your answers to these questions will show your understanding of the passage.

Here are some words you will need to know as you listen to the passage:

- **Holocaust**—the mass killing of approximately six million European Jews by the Nazis during World War II

- **Auschwitz**—a Nazi death camp where many Jews were murdered during World War II

The correct answers, with explanations, follow this test on pages 173–176.

CHILDREN'S BOOKS TRIUMPH OVER TRAGEDY

Alison Black

Margret and H. A. Rey, creators of the beloved *Curious George* books, first met when Margret (then, Margarete Waldstein) was a little girl sliding down the banisters of her family's home in Hamburg, Germany. Hans Reyersbach (H. A. Rey) was born in 1898. He lived near the Hagenbeck Zoo in Hamburg and loved to draw and paint many of the animals. In the 1920s, he traveled to Rio de Janiero, Brazil, to look for a job.

Margarete Waldstein was born in 1906. After Hitler's rise in Germany, she left Hamburg. In 1935, she too traveled to Rio, where the two met again. They married and became Brazilian citizens. Shortly after, Margarete changed her name to "Margret" and Hans changed his last name to "Rey." They did this to make their names simpler for Brazilians to pronounce. Their new citizenship and names would later save their lives.

The Reys sailed to Europe for their honeymoon. They settled in a Parisian neighborhood. It was there they began to write and illustrate children's books. In 1939, their first book, *Raffy and the Nine Monkeys*, was published. Then they began a story about the youngest monkey in *Raffy*, the one who was always getting into trouble. They called it *The Adventures of Fifi*.

That September, war between Germany and France broke out. By the following May, the Nazis had marched into Belgium and Holland. Refugees began pouring into Paris from the north. Hans used spare parts to build two bicycles. Margret gathered together their artwork and manuscripts. German planes flew overhead and the German army was just hours from Paris. In frantic haste, the couple joined millions of refugees heading south.

The Reys traveled slowly by bicycle. Although they were Jews, their Brazilian citizenship and their names made it easier for them to get visas. Once they were stopped and an official searched all their belongings. He had suspected they were spies because of their German accents. However, finding only children's stories and pictures, he allowed them to continue.

The Reys eventually made their way to Portugal and then to Rio de Janeiro. From there they sailed to New York City. Within five months, the couple had found a publisher for *The Adventures of Fifi*. However, the publisher insisted that Fifi was not a monkey's name, so the story of a mischievous little monkey became *Curious George*. It was published the next year. Just like Hans Reyersbach and his wife, Margarete Waldstein, Fifi, the little French monkey, changed his name and found freedom in the United States.

Another famous children's author and illustrator experienced World War II in a very different manner. Maurice Sendak, best known for his classics *Where the Wild Things Are* and *In the Night Kitchen*, was born in 1928 to Jewish immigrants. His family had come to the United States from Poland just before World War I. He grew up on the streets of Brooklyn, New York, and was fond of Mickey Mouse cartoons and movies such as *Fantasia* and *King Kong*.

When Sendak was thirteen, he was shocked to learn that his father's father, aunts, uncles, and cousins had all perished in the Holocaust. Images of fear and death appear in much of his work because of his family's loss. Marked by his need to deal with the Holocaust, Sendak's work is filled with a constant tension between horror and beauty. He has said that he writes to acknowledge those wild things, which shall always be untamed.

Brundibar is Sendak's most recent work. It is based on a 1938 children's opera by a Czech-Jewish composer, Hans Krasa. The opera tells the tale of two children who need money to buy milk for their ailing mother and are menaced by the bully Brundibar. Because of its symbolism, *Brundibar* represented resistance for the inmates of Terezin, a Nazi concentration camp. Children at the camp performed the opera fifty-five times. Unhappily, the composer and most of the performers were eventually sent to Auschwitz, where they died.

As Sendak's most overt treatment of the Holocaust, *Brundibar* echoes the author's constant theme of children learning how to be heroic in an adult world. Sendak may not mention World War II or even the Holocaust in his work, but as in *Brundibar*, there are clues, such as a Star of David on a coat lapel or a Hitler-style mustache on a bully.

The Reys personally experienced World War II. Making a horrific escape from occupied France, they were able to physically escape to a safer place. Their escape seems emotional as well. Despite their terrifying journey, the Reys created something simple and heart-warming for children, free of anger and fear. Maurice Sendak never directly experienced World War II. However, his memories of death and the Holocaust are played out in his stories and his art depicting children in danger; he is the boy Max who has tamed the Wild Things.

NOTES

NOTES

1. Although Margret and H. A. Rey originally met in Hamburg, Germany, in what country did they marry and get citizenship?

   A. France

   B. United States

   C. Portugal

   D. Brazil

2. Curious George is similar to his creators because

   A. he fled Paris by bicycle

   B. he changed his name and found freedom in the United States

   C. he was originally from Rio de Janiero, Brazil

   D. he always gets into trouble

3. Read the following sentences:

   When Sendak was thirteen, he was shocked to learn that his father's father, aunts, uncles, and cousins had all perished in the Holocaust. Images of fear and death appear in much of his work because of his family's loss.

   Based on these sentences, one can infer that Maurice Sendak

   A. did not know about this family tragedy until he was thirteen

   B. has used this tragedy as an inspiration for many of his books

   C. was forever saddened by his family's loss, even as an adult

   D. all of the above

4. The author's purpose for writing the article was **most likely** to

   A. explain the effects that World War II had on European Jews

   B. chronicle the lives of Margret and H. A. Rey and Maurice Sendak

   C. compare the effects of World War II on three children's book authors

   D. describe the children's books written by the Reys and Sendak

5. Which of the following sentences states the title of the children's book correctly?

    A. In 1939, their first book, *raffy and the nine monkeys,* was published.

    B. In 1939, their first book, "Raffy and the Nine Monkeys," was published.

    C. In 1939, their first book, *"Raffy and the Nine Monkeys,"* was published.

    D. In 1939, their first book, *Raffy and the Nine Monkeys,* was published.

6. Read the following sentence:

    Margret was a little girl sliding down the banisters of her family's home in Hamburg.

    Why is an apostrophe necessary in the word *family's?*

    A. It is a proper noun.

    B. It is a contraction.

    C. It is a possessive noun.

    D. It is a conjunction.

7. Which of the following sentences uses proper capitalization?

    A. By the following May, the nazis had marched into Belgium and Holland.

    B. By the following May, the Nazis had marched into Belgium and Holland.

    C. By the following May, the Nazis had marched into belgium and holland.

    D. By the following may, the nazis had marched into Belgium and Holland.

8. Read the following sentence:

   He was shocked to learn that his father's father, aunts, and cousins had all perished in the Holocaust.

   Why are commas used in this sentence?

   A. They separate a list of three things.

   B. They separate proper nouns.

   C. They separate possessive nouns.

   D. They divide up a complex sentence.

9. Margret and H. A. Rey and Maurice Sendak were affected by the events of World War II in different ways. In the chart below, list two effects that the authors dealt with.

Margret and H. A. Rey	Maurice Sendak

10. The struggle to survive and the tragedies of World War II changed the lives of these authors. How did the events of World War II affect the **stories** of Margret and H. A. Rey and Maurice Sendak? Explain what role the war had in shaping the stories of these authors. Use details from the passage to support your point.

   _____

   _____

   _____

   _____

   _____

   _____

11. Although the tragedies of World War II affected these authors in many different ways, the stories written by the Reys and Maurice Sendak have many similarities as well. What are some of the similarities between their children's books? Use details from the passage to explain these similarities.

_____

_____

_____

_____

_____

_____

BOOK 3: READING AND WRITING

4 Short-Response Questions

1 Extended-Response Question

60 Minutes to Complete—Work to the End of the Test.

Directions: Book 3 asks you to write about two passages you will read. When you write your responses, be sure to

- Clearly organize your ideas

- Clearly express your ideas

- Completely and accurately answer the questions

- Support the ideas in your responses with examples from the passage or passages and, if required by question, your experiences and opinions

- Make your writing enjoyable and interesting to the reader

One passage you will read is a short story by Scott Niven called "Obsession." It is about an elderly man's quest to sustain his immaculate lawn and yard despite the change of seasons. The other passage is a poem called "Another Spring" by C. Georgina Rosetti. In this poem, the narrator describes all the things she would do if she were to see spring again. Use what you learn from the passages to answer questions 1 through 5.

The correct answers, with explanations, follow this test on pages 176–180.

> **verdant**—1. covered with green; 2. immature or inexperienced.

OBSESSION

Scott Niven

Spencer maintained an immaculate yard.

His fastidiousness and attention to detail waited until his retirement to fully blossom. Then, with nothing to do but count age spots and wonder when his overeager son would sweep him into a nursing home, Spencer's mind turned to upkeep.

He bought a new rake. He planted exotic flowers. He purchased fertilizer, grass seed, and a riding lawn mower, then used the last of the three to keep the first two in line. Every blade of green measured three inches high. Every weed was plucked and burned, the ashes stuffed inside an airtight bag and driven to the dump. Sprinklers spun from four in the morning until five.

The town cancelled its Yard of the Month campaign. They awarded Spencer the sign permanently. He rigged wires to his house so the sign could hang above the lawn, thereby preserving his perfect greenway from puncture.

Despite his many landscaping accomplishments, however, Spencer cultivated a hatred for one relentless yearly foe.

Autumn.

From September to December, he spent his days raking leaves and cramming them into bags. Yet always upon returning from the dump, he discovered additional leaves scattered about the yard, mocking his impeccable fortress.

Eventually, Spencer fought back.

He bought a chain saw. One by one the great oaks fell. Pines crashed. Magnolias thudded. Dogwoods died.

September. Spencer watched the yard from his bay window. The jutting pencil points of truncated wood did not shed. But as the wind increased, leaves from his neighbors' trees stampeded onto his property, staining his pure and verdant grass. He rushed outside each time a new wave attacked, but the wind was ceaseless, and Spencer's body was not.

When he approached his neighbors, they declined the use of his chain saw. So he lugged the whirling, jagged teeth into a huge forest and left a much smaller forest in its stead. Then, with hammer, nails, and an abundance of timber, he erected a thirty-foot wall around the perimeter of his property. He draped the Yard of the Month sign on the outside of the wall to remind everyone what was inside.

October. Again Spencer fixated on the sparkling yard from his bay window.

November. Though his daily vigil continued, not a single, tainted leaf surmounted his spiked shield of wood.

December. Spencer began to relax. He limited his careful scrutiny to six hours a day.

Finally, one morning in early January, Spencer strolled across his yard, inhaling the sight of his victory. But as he gazed up at the northern wall, a furious wind billowed over its crest. A lone leaf fluttered through the air, flung itself over the spires, then drifted, drifted, drifted, eventually landing at Spencer's feet. Its diameter covered a two-inch swatch of his lovely, uncorrupted grass.

It was too much.

Spencer packed his bags and moved to Arizona.

1. In the chart that follows, identify how Spencer felt about each season. Support each feeling with details from the short story.

Spring	Summer
Feeling: Support from Passage:	Feeling: Support from Passage:
Autumn	Winter
Feeling: Support from Passage:	Feeling: Support from Passage:

2. What is the most convincing evidence in the short story that
Spencer might have developed an unhealthy obsession about his
yard? Explain why you chose the piece of evidence you did.

_____

_____

_____

_____

_____

_____

_____

_____

Mateless nightingales are said to sing during the night to attract a mate.

Mezereons are shrubs with fragrant, purple flowers.

ANOTHER SPRING

Christina Georgina Rossetti

If I might see another Spring
   I'd not plant summer flowers and wait:
I'd have my crocuses at once,
My leafless pink mezereons,
   My chill-veined snowdrops, choicer yet
   My white or azure violet,
Leaf-nested primrose; anything
   To blow at once, not late.

If I might see another Spring
   I'd listen to the daylight birds
That build their nests and pair and sing,
Not wait for mateless nightingale;
   I'd listen to the lusty herds,
   The ewes with lambs as white as snow,
I'd find out music in the hail
   And all the winds that blow.

If I might see another Spring—
   Oh stinging comment on my past
That all my past results in 'if'—
   If I might see another Spring
I'd laugh to-day, to-day is brief;
I would not wait for anything:
   I'd use to-day that cannot last,
   Be glad to-day and sing.

3. How do we know from the poem that the narrator is feeling a sense of urgency, as if she cannot wait for Spring? Select and interpret phrases from the poem that support this feeling of immediacy to complete the chart below.

First Stanza	Second Stanza	Third Stanza
Evidence: Interpretation:	Evidence: Interpretation:	Evidence: Interpretation:

4. What do you think the poet's purpose is for writing this poem? Support your response with details from the poem.

_____

_____

_____

_____

_____

_____

_____

PLANNING PAGE

You may PLAN your writing for question 5 on this page. Write your final response on the lines on the next pages.

5. Spencer in "Obsession" and the narrator in the poem "Another Spring" both have very strong perspectives on the change of seasons. From what you know about Spencer and the narrator through these two passages, describe how each views the change of seasons. Then, if the two were to meet, tell how the narrator of the poem might persuade Spencer to look at the change of seasons from her perspective.

In your answer, be sure to

■ describe how Spencer views the change of seasons;

■ describe how the poem's narrator views the change of seasons;

■ tell how the poem's narrator might persuade Spencer to look at seasons from the narrator's perspective;

■ include details from both passages to support your response;

■ check your grammar, spelling, and punctuation.

_____

_____

_____

_____

_____

_____

_____

_____

_____

_____

_____

_____

_____

_____

_____

_____

_____

_____

_____

_____

_____

_____

_____

_____

_____

_____

_____

_____

_____

_____

_____

_____

_____

_____

_____

ANSWERS AND EXPLANATIONS

BOOK 1: READING

"Was Mark Twain a Naturalist?"

1. **D** Mark Twain was a false name Samuel Clemens used to identify himself as the author of the books he wrote. Pen names are similar to stage names (when actors change their real names for various reasons).

2. **A** If the definition of a naturalist is someone who studies nature, choice A comes closest to including that definition in its description. A naturalist is more than someone who just travels to different places.

3. **C** Although the other choices are touched upon in the passage, the main topic informs the reader about Mark Twain.

4. **C** This response is the only one that connects Twain's adventures with his writing.

"A Minor Bird"

5. **B** The poem is written in past tense, so it has to be by someone who watched a bird in the past. In the poem, "I" is a person talking about a bird.

6. **A** Choice A is the only response that can be supported by these two lines alone.

7. **D** The phrase "any song" indicates that the author is referring not only to birds but perhaps to the songs (voices) of some people.

Excerpt from *How the Leopard Got His Spots*

8. **A** These are all examples of similes because they compare two things that are not alike in most ways but are similar in one important way.

9. **B** While dark places, hunting, zebras, and giraffes are mentioned in the excerpt, most of the story is about the Leopard getting his spots so he can be a better hunter.

10. **D** By setting off Best Beloved with a comma, the author indicates that the person telling the story is talking to someone. It seems that the storyteller or author is sharing this story with a loved one.

11. **D** The author tells us that Baviaan offered advice to the Ethiopian and the Leopard, but we are not told who Baviaan is.

12. **A** The main idea of the excerpt is that the Ethiopian and the Leopard change their skin so they can be camouflaged and blend in with the colors of the jungle, or the "background." Being camouflaged will improve their chances of catching their prey because they will be able to get closer to their prey before being noticed.

13. **B** The only sentence that connects hunting with friendship is choice B.

14. **D** It is most likely this conversation occurs in the jungle because the types of animals included—leopard, giraffe, and zebra—are typically jungle animals. It more than likely is not a zoo, even though these animals could be found there also, because the animals are concerned with hunting.

"Then There Were Three . . . An Elephant Tale"

15. **C** The quotation marks around "younger" indicate the author is using the term loosely because she is talking about being young in a relative way. When you're referring to being millions of years older or younger, the word *young* seems contradictory.

16. **C** A family tree illustrates familial lines or one's ancestors. Choice C says the Asian elephant's tree goes further back than the mammoth's tree does.

17. **A** Ending with the paragraph about elephants becoming extinct due to human behavior has a gloomy effect.

18. **D** Although the author says in the passage that the tusks were probably the cause of the mammoth's extinction, she does not say why or what about the tusks was the cause.

19. **D** This fact is stated directly in the passage among all of the details.

20. **A** The other choices are not correct statements based on the passage; the only accurate choice is A.

"Computers in Our Lives"

21. **C** There is evidence to support that the author believes computers are helpful to humans, but there is no evidence to support the other choices.

22. **C** While there is some information on Bill Gates and Microsoft Windows, most of the passage is about how computers have transformed our everyday lives. There is no information on various types of computers.

23. **B** You have to be a very careful reader to get this answer correct. All of the choices appear in the passage, but the only one that is directly connected to the Computer Age is choice B.

24. **C** The question refers to Windows. The passage said Windows was developed by Gates at Microsoft, so the best place to look for the answer to this question is on page 68.

25. **A** Although the other answers may be true, the only reason the author provides that an electronic thermostat is a computer is that it can be programmed.

26. **A** By saying Gates made PCs user-friendly, he is implying they previously were not accessible to amateur users.

27. **A** All the other statements are true, but using computers to find information quickly is the only choice that shows how computers can save time.

28. **C** It is true that only the wealthy owned computers in the 1980s. However, this does not demonstrate how computers are more user friendly today.

"Words"

29. **A** The poem is written in three stanzas, has a rhyme scheme, and includes imagery; therefore, the only answer that is not represented in the poem is free verse.

30. **B** Personification and simile are both represented in the poem. The forms of figurative language mentioned in the other choices are not present.

31. **D** *Influential* means *powerful*. The poem focuses on the idea that the words one utters can become reality, so one must use positive words over negative ones. Thus, *influential* is an appropriate word because it describes the power words can have.

32. **C** *Space* is a synonym for the word *realm*.

33. **A** *Caution* is the tone because the author instructs the reader to "be careful of their use" and the effects words can have in one's life.

"The Fox and the Goat"

34. **D** *Hiding* is a synonym for concealing.

35. **B** *Gullible* describes the goat best because he is referred to as being "thoughtless" and "mindful of only his thirst." The word *gullible* is defined as "easy to fool," and this fits the description of the way the goat behaves.

36. **A** *Scolded* is a synonym for *upbraided*. This is exactly what the goat does to the fox when he realizes he has been tricked and cannot get out of the well.

37. **C** The goat was very thirsty, and when the fox described how the water was "excellent beyond measure," he jumped in. The goat was not thinking about how he would get out of the well once he took a drink.

38. **A** The moral is "look before you leap" because the goat did not "look" or think of the consequences before he jumped into the well.

Excerpt from Helen Keller's Autobiography

39. **C** Helen states that in the beginning she was simply imitating Miss Sullivan's hand movements. She did not connect any meaning to them.

40. **A** Miss Sullivan is determined. Although Helen doesn't understand what the movements mean in the beginning, Miss Sullivan knows that if she keeps spelling the word in Helen's hand after she has contact with the water, a connection between the two will develop. Through Miss Sullivan's determination, Helen learns the connection between words and what they represent.

41. **D** All of the lessons mentioned apply to this instance between Helen and Miss Sullivan.

BOOK 2: LISTENING AND WRITING MECHANICS

"Children's Books Triumph Over Tragedy"

1. **C** Although they lived in or visited all the other countries mentioned, Brazil was where they married and gained citizenship.

2. **B** Curious George was originally called Fifi when his story was published in France. His name was changed to George when the Reys made it safely to the United States and got the story published.

3. **D** All of the statements are accurate.

4. **C** Although the passage discusses sections of the authors' lives, as well as portions of their books, the main purpose is the comparison of the effects the war had on the authors.

5. **D** Book titles are underlined or italicized. Short works, such as poems or short stories, have quotation marks around the title.

No titles receive both quotation marks and underlining. All titles should be capitalized because they are proper nouns.

6. **C** The phrase *family's home* is possessive, showing the reader that the home is owned by the family.

7. **B** The words *May, Nazis, Belgium,* and *Holland* are all proper nouns. This means they need to be capitalized.

8. **A** Whenever a series of three or more things are listed, commas must be used to separate them.

9. Your graphic organizer should resemble the following, listing two effects of World War II that the authors dealt with.

Margret and H. A. Rey	Maurice Sendak
Forced to flee Paris on bicycles to avoid the approaching Nazis.	Discovered when he was thirteen that his entire family on his father's side was killed during the Holocaust.
Fear of not being able to leave France because they were Jewish.	Even as an adult, needed to deal with his loss by including the images of horror in his writings.
Stopped and searched on their way out of the country because of their German accents.	Used symbolism in many of his children's books to represent the fear that many dealt with both during and after the Holocaust.
Left their home to settle in the United States.	

10. The short response should use details from the passage to explain the role the war had in shaping the stories of these authors. It should resemble the following:

The events of World War II had a direct effect on the stories of the Reys and Maurice Sendak. Margret and H. A. Rey were Jewish, so they had to flee Paris when the Nazis were getting ready to take over. Although they were stopped and searched, they were allowed to leave the country with their stories because they were Brazilian citizens. Because they were able to escape, Curious George was able to have his story told in America. However, Maurice Sendak found out that everyone from his father's side of the family was killed during the Holocaust, and it changed the way he looked at the world. His children's stories often show children in danger, similar to the danger and fear that his relatives faced during the Holocaust. He says his work has a tension between horror and beauty, which helps him deal with the tragedies of the Holocaust.

11. The short response should use details from the passage to describe the similarities between the children's books written by Margret and H.A. Rey and Maurice Sendak. It should resemble the following:

The authors Margret and H.A. Rey and Maurice Sendak are both famous for their children's stories. The main characters in Curious George and Where the Wild Things Are are similar in that they all overcome difficult situations. Although George always gets into trouble, he always finds a way out of it. Also, Max is able to tame the monsters and avoid danger in <u>Where the Wild Things Are</u>. Therefore, the personal strength of these three authors is reflected in the strength of the characters in their children's books.

Another possible similarity to mention is the strength of the children in *Brundibar*. Also, the main characters in all of these stories are young, and yet they survive in harsh worlds. For example, George is a little monkey in the world of people, Max is in a world of monsters, and the children in *Brundibar* have to outsmart a bully.

BOOK 3: READING AND WRITING

"Obsession"

1. The graphic organizer should be completed with details directly from the passage. Here are some of the possible answers.

Spring	Summer
Feeling: Spencer liked Spring.	Feeling: Spencer liked Summer.
Support from Passage: He was proud of the fact that he got the Yard of the Month sign to keep on his lawn.	Support from Passage: There isn't a separate description of how he felt about Summer. We can probably safely assume Spring and Summer feelings were the same. Watering his lawn probably referred to summer care, though. He seemed happy about watering his lawn for one hour each day.

Autumn	Winter
Feeling: Spencer was aggravated and frustrated with Autumn.	Feeling: Spencer liked it until January when the leaf blew over the fence he had built.
Support from Passage: The author calls Autumn Spencer's "relentless yearly foe." He didn't like the leaves falling on his lawn. He kept watch for leaves and went out and picked them up when he saw them until he finally chopped down the trees in his yard and put up a fence to keep his neighbors' leaves from stampeding into his yard.	Support from Passage: The lone leaf was the straw that broke the camel's back. He decided to move to Arizona to escape lawn care.

2. The short response to this question should be similar to the following:

The most convincing evidence that Spencer had developed an unhealthy obsession with his lawn and yard was that Spencer built the thirty-foot fence after his neighbors refused the use of his chainsaw to cut down their trees. The height of the fence was extraordinary (thirty feet!) and is proof that he had developed an unhealthy obsession about his lawn. Also, it was extravagant that he cut the trees and lumber to build the fence on his own when, supposedly, he was an elderly retired man with nothing else to think about.

Other possible responses might be that he ran outside and picked up the leaves each time they fell or that he cut down all of the trees in his yard.

"Another Spring"

3. The graphic organizer should be completed with details directly from the passage. Here are some of the possible answers.

First Stanza	Second Stanza	Third Stanza
Evidence: The author writes, "I'd not plant summer flowers and wait." Interpretation: The narrator wants to enjoy the flowers that come up right away, like the crocuses, and not wait for the flowers that bloom later in the Summer.	Evidence: The author says she will "Not wait for mate-less nightin-gale." Interpretation: The narrator will enjoy the birds that sing in the day and not wait for mate-less nightin-gales who sing at night. So, she doesn't even want to wait until nighttime in the Spring to hear birds sing.	Evidence: The author "would not wait for anything." Interpretation: The narrator states her urgency outright by saying this. She would laugh and enjoy today because it is so brief. She would live and enjoy life as it happens.

4. The short response to this question should be similar to the following:

It is most likely the author wrote this poem to express the urgency people feel when they find out they are ill and may not live long enough to see the change of seasons. Maybe the author herself is dying. She keeps saying "if" as if she is unsure whether or not she will live long enough to see the next Spring come. Also, she ends the poem talking about enjoying today. That makes one think she isn't sure if she has many "tomorrows."

Other feasible responses might be that the author wants to portray someone who is experiencing a long, cold Winter and can't wait until the warmth of Spring or someone who has lost a love and is talking about Spring as if it represents hope of a new love.

5. Your answer should be similar to the response that follows:

Spencer in "Obsession" looks at the changing of the seasons with apprehension and trepidation. He worries about what each season will bring to harm his "pure and verdant grass." The story says he "cultivated a hatred for one relentless yearly foe," which was Autumn. He was "fixated on the sparkling yard" for hours a day to ensure it was safe from leaves and weeds. His obsession kept him from enjoying life day to day.

The narrator of the poem "Another Spring," on the other hand, is looking forward to enjoying another Spring. She is hopeful that she will be able to enjoy the flowers and the birds. Her attitude is one of hope rather than apprehension. She wouldn't sit around waiting for anything but instead would "use to-day that cannot last." The narrator wants to enjoy life day to day.

If Spencer and the narrator of the poem were to meet, the narrator might persuade Spencer to look at the change of seasons from her perspective by helping him look at the positive possibilities as she does in her poem. She might persuade him to get out and enjoy life day to day instead of sitting around worrying about his lawn all day long. Spencer sounds like he is an elderly, retired man who may not see many more springs. The narrator could persuade him to think about that and help him find other interests to occupy his mind and time. The narrator might help Spencer become more involved with his family or neighbors so he isn't home alone all of the time "counting age spots" and wondering when his "overeager son would sweep him into a nursing home." Maybe she could persuade him to get interested in something that would satisfy his "fastidiousness and attention to detail," such as painting or writing. The narrator might help Spencer in many ways if she could persuade him to look positively at things.

PRACTICE TEST 2

TIPS TO DO YOUR BEST

- Carefully read all the directions.
- Plan how you will use your time wisely.
- Read each question thoroughly.
- Before choosing your response, think about the answer.

BOOK 1: READING

41 Multiple-Choice Questions

70 Minutes to Complete—Work Until You Come to Book 2.

DIRECTIONS

In Book 1, you will read eight or more passages and answer several questions about each one. Fill in the answers to the multiple-choice questions on the bubble sheet on the next page. You may make notes or marks on the test pages as you read. Be sure to answer all of the questions. The correct answers, with explanations, follow this test on pages 223–227.

ANSWER SHEET

Short-response questions in Book 2 and all questions in Book 3 should be answered directly on the test pages.

BOOK 1

1. Ⓐ Ⓑ Ⓒ Ⓓ   15. Ⓐ Ⓑ Ⓒ Ⓓ   29. Ⓐ Ⓑ Ⓒ Ⓓ
2. Ⓐ Ⓑ Ⓒ Ⓓ   16. Ⓐ Ⓑ Ⓒ Ⓓ   30. Ⓐ Ⓑ Ⓒ Ⓓ
3. Ⓐ Ⓑ Ⓒ Ⓓ   17. Ⓐ Ⓑ Ⓒ Ⓓ   31. Ⓐ Ⓑ Ⓒ Ⓓ
4. Ⓐ Ⓑ Ⓒ Ⓓ   18. Ⓐ Ⓑ Ⓒ Ⓓ   32. Ⓐ Ⓑ Ⓒ Ⓓ
5. Ⓐ Ⓑ Ⓒ Ⓓ   19. Ⓐ Ⓑ Ⓒ Ⓓ   33. Ⓐ Ⓑ Ⓒ Ⓓ
6. Ⓐ Ⓑ Ⓒ Ⓓ   20. Ⓐ Ⓑ Ⓒ Ⓓ   34. Ⓐ Ⓑ Ⓒ Ⓓ
7. Ⓐ Ⓑ Ⓒ Ⓓ   21. Ⓐ Ⓑ Ⓒ Ⓓ   35. Ⓐ Ⓑ Ⓒ Ⓓ
8. Ⓐ Ⓑ Ⓒ Ⓓ   22. Ⓐ Ⓑ Ⓒ Ⓓ   36. Ⓐ Ⓑ Ⓒ Ⓓ
9. Ⓐ Ⓑ Ⓒ Ⓓ   23. Ⓐ Ⓑ Ⓒ Ⓓ   37. Ⓐ Ⓑ Ⓒ Ⓓ
10. Ⓐ Ⓑ Ⓒ Ⓓ   24. Ⓐ Ⓑ Ⓒ Ⓓ   38. Ⓐ Ⓑ Ⓒ Ⓓ
11. Ⓐ Ⓑ Ⓒ Ⓓ   25. Ⓐ Ⓑ Ⓒ Ⓓ   39. Ⓐ Ⓑ Ⓒ Ⓓ
12. Ⓐ Ⓑ Ⓒ Ⓓ   26. Ⓐ Ⓑ Ⓒ Ⓓ   40. Ⓐ Ⓑ Ⓒ Ⓓ
13. Ⓐ Ⓑ Ⓒ Ⓓ   27. Ⓐ Ⓑ Ⓒ Ⓓ   41. Ⓐ Ⓑ Ⓒ Ⓓ
14. Ⓐ Ⓑ Ⓒ Ⓓ   28. Ⓐ Ⓑ Ⓒ Ⓓ

BOOK 2

1. Ⓐ Ⓑ Ⓒ Ⓓ   4. Ⓐ Ⓑ Ⓒ Ⓓ   7. Ⓐ Ⓑ Ⓒ Ⓓ
2. Ⓐ Ⓑ Ⓒ Ⓓ   5. Ⓐ Ⓑ Ⓒ Ⓓ   8. Ⓐ Ⓑ Ⓒ Ⓓ
3. Ⓐ Ⓑ Ⓒ Ⓓ   6. Ⓐ Ⓑ Ⓒ Ⓓ

Directions: Read the following poem by Carl Sandburg.
Then answer questions 1 through 4.

ARITHMETIC

Carl Sandburg

Arithmetic is where numbers fly like pigeons in and out of your head.

Arithmetic tells you how many you lose or win if you know how many you had before you lost or won.

Arithmetic is seven eleven all good children go to heaven—or five six bundle of sticks.

Arithmetic is numbers you squeeze from your head to your hand to your pencil to your paper till you get the answer.

Arithmetic is where the answer is right and everything is nice and you can look out of the window and see the blue sky—or the answer is wrong and you have to start all over and try again and see how it comes out this time.

If you take a number and double it and double it again and then double it a few more times, the number gets bigger and bigger and goes higher and higher and only arithmetic can tell you what the number is when you decide to quit doubling.

Arithmetic is where you have to multiply—and you carry the multiplication table in your head and hope you won't lose it.

If you have two animal crackers, one good and one bad, and you eat one and a striped zebra with streaks all over him eats the other, how many animal crackers will you have if somebody offers you five six seven and you say No no no and you say Nay nay nay and you say Nix nix nix?

1. Read the following sentence from the poem:

   Arithmetic is numbers you squeeze from your head to your hand to your pencil to your paper till you get the answer.

   What image does the author create?

   A. a student struggling to solve an arithmetic problem

   B. a student writing a list of numbers

   C. a student using a calculator

   D. a student doing an arithmetic problem on a chalkboard

2. Which sentence from the poem best supports the feeling that arithmetic is stressful for the author?

   A. Arithmetic is seven eleven all good children go to heaven—or five six bundle of sticks.

   B. Arithmetic is where numbers fly like pigeons in and out of your head.

   C. If you take a number and double it and double it again and then double it a few more times, the number gets bigger and bigger and goes higher and higher and only arithmetic can tell you what the number is when you decide to quit doubling.

   D. Arithmetic is where you have to multiply—and you carry the multiplication table in your head and hope you won't lose it.

3. Which of the following sentences from the poem is a simile?

   A. Arithmetic is where numbers fly like pigeons in and out of your head.

   B. Arithmetic tells you how many you lose or win if you know how many you had before you lost or won.

   C. Arithmetic is seven eleven all good children go to heaven—or five six bundle of sticks.

   D. If you ask your mother for one fried egg for breakfast and she gives you two fried eggs and you eat both of them, who is better in arithmetic, you or your mother?

4. Read the following sentence from the poem:

   If you have two animal crackers, one good and one bad, and you eat one and a striped zebra with streaks all over him eats the other, how many animal crackers will you have if somebody offers you five six seven and you say No no no and you say Nay nay nay and you say Nix nix nix?

   This sentence implies that the speaker is in what mood?

   A. relaxed

   B. frustrated

   C. melancholy

   D. nostalgic

Directions: Read this excerpt from a short story by Lou Paduano.
Then answer questions 5 through 7.

Feeling the shadows around her, she surrendered. Racing back to the closet, she
grabbed her boots and threw a coat on over her bathrobe before heading out into
the darkness.

Betsy found them at the edge of the bluff. He sat, his legs dangling over the abrupt
drop to the Atlantic, staring out at the waves crashing against the shadowy beach
below. Autumn sat beside him, the content Husky, nurtured by the constant rubbing
behind his ear from the caressing fingers of his owner. Light began to creep in before
them. The storm had ended and a new day was approaching. The thought brought little
comfort to Betsy as she sat next to the man she would have called husband a thousand
times over. The man she lived for and through for the better part of her life.

He didn't say a word. His eyes never left the horizon and the rising of the sun. Betsy
knew there were few words left.

"They're going through with the test, aren't they?" she asked. The words crept from
her lips and hung between them in the thick, dewy air of the morning. They clung to the
damp air that had remained behind the large storm clouds that were now out of sight,
echoing through the cliff and repeating against the onslaught of the ocean waves.

He nodded in silence. His hand dropped away from Autumn's ear and fell against
his other palm. His fingers interlaced and his thumbs tapped together in rhythm with
his heartbeat. Slowly. Thoughtfully. Betsy never claimed to be as brilliant as the man
beside her, but she had heard enough from Horace and the sporadic calls to know
what was about to occur. What she had always known would occur.

"Is there any chance it won't work?" she found herself asking, praying for an answer
that could never be given. "A chance that you're wrong about the whole thing?"

"No," he whispered, still staring out into the distance. More light reached above the
horizon, illuminating the deep blue hues of the ocean and the sky above it.

Betsy sat, silent, her hands in her lap. She wanted to reach for him. She wanted to
pull him close, to learn more; but she stopped herself short of taking action. All her life
had built up to this moment. This single moment with the man she loved. It could only
end this way.

"When?" That was all she could ask. Out of all of the questions burning in her mind,
it was the only relevant one left.

"Any minute now." The tapping of his thumbs stopped; his hands fell to his sides.
Stretching out, his fingers found hers, sliding along her cool skin and tightly gripping her.
His hands locked with hers, his thumbs rubbing against the back of her hands slowly.
Then Horace lifted Betsy's tired eyes until they met his own. She stared deeply into the
soul of the man she had loved and hated more than anything in the world. She reflected

on everything they had built together, the pain, the love, the hope, and the sacrifices. This was the only way it could end for them, for Horace and the device he had been working on since the first days of their relationship. Betsy thought of all of the loneliness that came from the calls that took Horace away from her for weeks at a time.

As the light suddenly exploded before them and spread in every direction, sending the final shockwave over the waves toward their small cabin on the bluffs, Betsy saw the true face of the man before her. She saw the smile that spread across the face of Horace Winter as he held tightly to her hand.

5. What might be the **best** title for this short story, based on what we know about the story from this excerpt?

    A. An Ocean Getaway

    B. One Dreaded Moment

    C. Betsy's Sacrifices

    D. Nuclear Science

6. What will **most likely** happen to Betsy and Horace next?

    A. They will die from a second explosion.

    B. They will run away scared.

    C. They will both jump off the cliff.

    D. They will return to their small cabin on the bluffs.

7. Read this sentence from the passage:

    She saw the smile that spread across the face of Horace Winter as he held tightly to her hand.

    In this sentence, the author

    A. allows readers to interpret Horace's character and motivation

    B. tells readers Horace is proud of his work

    C. tells readers Horace is glad his work is done

    D. shows Betsy and Horace feel the same way about the explosion

Directions: Read this fable. Then answer questions 8 through 13.

THE THIEF AND THE INNKEEPER

A thief hired a room in a tavern and stayed a while in the hope of stealing something that would enable him to pay his reckoning. When he had waited some days in vain, he saw the innkeeper dressed in a new and handsome coat and sitting before his door. The thief sat down beside him and talked with him. As the conversation began to flag, the thief yawned terribly and at the same time howled like a wolf.

The innkeeper said, "Why do you howl so fearfully?"

"I will tell you," said the thief, "but first let me ask you to hold my clothes, or I shall tear them to pieces. I know not, sir, when I got this habit of yawning. Neither do I know whether these attacks of howling were inflicted on me as a judgment for my crimes or for any other cause. But, this I do know: When I yawn for the third time, I actually turn into a wolf and attack men."

With this speech he commenced a second fit of yawning and again howled like a wolf, as he had at first. The innkeeper, hearing the thief's tale and believing what he said, became greatly alarmed and, rising from his seat, attempted to run away.

The thief laid hold of his coat and entreated him to stop, saying, "Pray wait, sir, and hold my clothes, or I shall tear them to pieces in my fury, when I turn into a wolf." At the same moment he yawned the third time and sent up a terrible howl. The innkeeper, frightened lest he should be attacked, left his new coat in the thief's hand and ran as fast as he could into the inn for safety. The thief made off with the coat and did not return again to the inn.

8. Read this sentence from the fable:

   The thief laid hold of his coat and entreated him to stop, saying, "Pray wait, sir, and hold my clothes, or I shall tear them to pieces in my fury, when I turn into a wolf."

   The word *entreated* means about the same as

   A. grabbed

   B. insulted

   C. pleaded with

   D. demanded

9. According to the fable, the innkeeper ran away because

   A. the thief was robbing him

   B. he was afraid he was going to get attacked

   C. the thief gave him his clothes

   D. the thief was insane

10. What would be the **best** moral for this fable?

    A. Every tale is not to be believed.

    B. Older is wiser.

    C. A penny saved is a penny earned.

    D. A bird in hand is worth two in the bush.

11. The fable is told from the point of view of

    A. the wolf

    B. the innkeeper

    C. the thief

    D. the author

12. Overall, the innkeeper can be described as

    A. friendly

    B. ignorant

    C. selfish

    D. angry

13. Read this sentence from the passage:

    As the conversation began to flag, the thief yawned terribly and at the same time howled like a wolf.

    Now read the dictionary entry below.

    flag *v.* 1. to mark or decorate 2. to send a message 3. to signal 4. to droop or lose interest

    Which definition is closest to the meaning of *flag* as it is used in the sentence above?

    A. definition 1

    B. definition 2

    C. definition 3

    D. definition 4

14. In the last paragraph, what image does the reader get from the author's description?

    A. the thief wrestling with the innkeeper to steal his coat

    B. the innkeeper wiggling his way out of the coat to run away as the thief securely holds onto the coat

    C. the thief politely holding the coat as the innkeeper takes it off

    D. the innkeeper handing the coat to the thief

Directions: Read this excerpt from *Black Beauty, Young Folks' Edition* by Anna Sewell. Then answer questions 15 through 20.

The first place that I can well remember was a pleasant meadow with a pond of clear water in it. Over the hedge on one side we looked into a plowed field, and on the other we looked over a gate at our master's house, which stood by the roadside. While I was young, I lived upon my mother's milk as I could not eat grass. In the daytime I ran by her side, and at night I lay down close by her. When it was hot, we used to stand by the pond in the shade of the trees. When it was cold, we had a warm shed near the grove.

There were six young colts in the meadow beside me. They were older than I was. I used to run with them and had great fun. We used to gallop all together around the field, as hard as we could go. Sometimes we had rather rough play, for they would bite and kick, as well as gallop.

One day, when there was a good deal of kicking, my mother whinnied to me to come to her. She said, "I wish you to pay attention to what I am going to say. The colts who live here are very good colts, but they are cart-horse colts. They have not learned manners. You have been well-bred and well-born. Your father has a great name in these parts, and your grandfather won the cup at the races. Your grandmother had the sweetest temper of any horse I ever knew, and I think you have never seen me kick or bite. I hope you will grow up gentle and good. Never learn bad ways. Do your work with a good will. Lift your feet up well when you trot, and never bite or kick even in play."

I have never forgotten my mother's advice. I knew she was a wise old horse, and our master thought a great deal of her. Her name was Duchess, but he called her Pet.

15. This passage is told from the point of view of

   A. Black Beauty

   B. Black Beauty's mother

   C. the master

   D. Black Beauty's friend

16. What is the passage **mostly** about?

   A. a mother's advice

   B. six young colts

   C. Black Beauty's early home

   D. the master's horses

17. What does Black Beauty's "first place" most likely represent to him?

    A. being trained

    B. growing up

    C. early hardships

    D. new freedom

18. Which statement from the passage best shows how he feels about his mother?

    A. I have never forgotten my mother's advice.

    B. I knew she was a wise old horse, and our master thought a great deal of her.

    C. Her name was Duchess, but he called her Pet.

    D. While I was young, I lived upon my mother's milk as I could not eat grass.

19. The author's description of Black Beauty's first place helps to create a sense of

    A. sadness

    B. tension

    C. peacefulness

    D. anticipation

20. Black Beauty's mother expects him to

    A. grow up kind and be proud

    B. beat all of the other colts when they play

    C. stop playing with the other colts

    D. tend to her needs

Directions: Read this passage. Then answer questions 21 through 28.

PRESIDENT BARACK OBAMA: AN EMERGING LEADER

Anuradhaa Shastri ·

Barack Obama is the 44th president of the United States. He is the first African American to hold this post. His varied and rich personal and professional background and experiences have helped to prepare him for this powerful and demanding position.

Barack Obama was born in Hawaii on August 4, 1961. His father was from Kenya and his mother from Kansas. His parents met at the University of Hawaii. His mother was a student there, and his father had won a scholarship that allowed him to leave Kenya and pursue his dreams in America.

Obama's father eventually returned to Kenya after completing his studies, and Obama was raised by his mother and grandparents in Hawaii. Through his childhood years, he struggled to find answers about his multicultural, multiracial heritage. As a very small child, he found it difficult to accept such vast differences between his mother's and father's skin color.

After high school, Obama moved to Los Angeles and studied at the Occidental College for two years. He then went to Columbia College in New York and majored in political science with a specialization in international relations. After completing his studies and working in New York for some time, he moved back to Chicago, where he was hired as a community organizer by the Developing Communities Project, a church-based community organization. The organization wanted a young black man to help it collaborate with black churches on the South Side of Chicago. He helped black people fight for their rights from the city government. He worked to improve the living conditions of poor neighborhoods that faced high rates of crime and unemployment. Working in a small organization taught him organizational skills.

During this time, Barack Obama decided law was a medium that could facilitate activism and community organization. So, in 1988, he entered Harvard Law School in Boston, Massachusetts. In his second year in college, he became editor-in-chief of a law review journal. He supervised a journal staff of about 80 editors. After he graduated from Harvard, he moved back to Chicago, where he practiced as a civil rights lawyer. He also taught constitutional law at the University of Chicago Law School from 1992 to 2004.

In the 1992 presidential election, he organized Project Vote, the largest voter registration drive in the history of Chicago. With a staff of 10 and more than 700 volunteers, Project Vote set a goal to register 150,000 unregistered African-American voters in the state of Illinois. Obama's work on Project Vote led him to run for the Illinois State Senate. He was elected and served three terms.

Obama declared his candidacy for the 2008 Democratic presidential nomination in February 2007 at the Old State Capitol building in Springfield, Illinois. In August 2008, he accepted the nomination of the Democratic Party and prepared to run against the Republican nominee, John McCain.

As they say, the rest is history! Obama is currently serving his first term as President of the United States of America. He was awarded the 2009 Nobel Peace Prize for his extraordinary efforts to strengthen collaboration and diplomacy among nations worldwide. What is next for this emerging leader?

21. The author's purpose for writing this passage was **most likely** to

    A. support Obama's nomination and encourage American citizens to vote for him

    B. persuade Republicans to support Obama

    C. inform readers of Obama's background

    D. boast about Obama's civil rights work in Chicago

22. Why did the author **most likely** include information about Obama's childhood?

    A. because it is interesting

    B. to demonstrate Obama's views and goals as a politician and person

    C. to show he is a great leader

    D. to show he will be a successful president

23. According to this passage, why did Obama go to law school?

    A. His parents wanted him to go into law.

    B. He wanted to follow in his father's footsteps.

    C. He got a scholarship to Harvard Law School.

    D. He thought it would help him make changes.

24. Which sentence **best** supports the main idea of the passage?

    A. As they say, the rest is history!

    B. Barack Obama is the 44th president of the United States.

    C. His varied and rich personal and professional background and experiences have helped to prepare him for this powerful and demanding position.

    D. His parents met at the University of Hawaii.

25. What does the author mean by the phrase "declared his candidacy"?

    A. Obama confirmed he would be a presidential candidate and run for the office.

    B. Obama nominated himself to be President.

    C. Obama confirmed he would take the job as President.

    D. Obama stated he would not be President.

26. The information in this passage would be **most** useful to someone who is writing a research paper about

    A. the Illinois State Senate

    B. Barack Obama

    C. multiracial families

    D. Project Vote

27. One experience from Obama's personal life that **most likely** helped prepare him for his presidential position was

    A. he moved frequently as a young adult

    B. as a child, he lived with his grandparents

    C. he came to terms with his multicultural heritage

    D. he learned his father was from Kenya

28. The professional experience that **best** demonstrates that Obama is interested in promoting civil rights is

   A. his work as a community organizer

   B. his job as senator for Illinois

   C. his organization of Project Vote

   D. his teaching career at a law school

Directions: Read this poem by Horatio Alger, Jr. Then answer questions 29 through 32.

MY CASTLE

Horatio Alger, Jr.

I have a beautiful castle,
With towers and battlements fair;
And many a banner, with gay device,
Floats in the outer air.

The walls are of solid silver;
The towers are of massive gold;
And the lights that stream from the windows
A royal scene unfold.

Ah! could you but enter my castle
With its pomp of regal sheen,
You would say that it far surpasses
The palace of Aladeen.

Could you but enter as I do,
And pace through the vaulted hall,
And mark the stately columns,
And the pictures on the wall;

With the costly gems about them,
That send their light afar,
With a chaste and softened splendor
Like the light of a distant star!

And where is this wonderful castle,
With its rich emblazonings,
Whose pomp so far surpasses
The homes of the greatest kings?

Come out with me at morning
And lie in the meadow-grass,
And lift your eyes to the ether blue,
And you will see it pass.

There! can you not see the battlements;
And the turrets stately and high,
Whose lofty summits are tipped with clouds,
And lost in the arching sky?

Dear friend, you are only dreaming,
Your castle so stately and fair
Is only a fanciful structure,—
A castle in the air.

Perchance you are right. I know not
If a phantom it may be;
But yet, in my inmost heart, I feel
That it lives, and lives for me.

For when clouds and darkness are round me,
And my heart is heavy with care,
I steal me away from the noisy crowd,
To dwell in my castle fair.

There are servants to do my bidding;
There are servants to heed my call;
And I, with a master's air of pride,
May pace through the vaulted hall.

And I envy not the monarchs
With cities under their sway;
For am I not, in my own right,
A monarch as proud as they?

What matter, then, if to others
My castle a phantom may be,
Since I feel, in the depths of my own heart,
That it is not so to me?

29. The castle being described is **most likely**

    A. a cloud formation

    B. a hallucination

    C. a dream

    D. a storm

30. The reader can infer that the narrator loves the castle because

    A. it is enormous and elegant

    B. it makes him feel like a monarch

    C. it has servants to wait on him

    D. thinking of it lifts his spirits

31. Read the following stanza,

> **What matter, then, if to others**
> **My castle a phantom may be,**
> **Since I feel, in the depths of my own heart,**
> **That it is not so to me?**

In these lines, the narrator is saying

    A. it is important that others believe in his castle

    B. her castle is a figment of his imagination

    C. it only matters that the castle is real to him

    D. the castle exists in his heart

32. The mood of this poem could be described as

    A. mournful

    B. contented

    C. unfulfilled

    D. hostile

Directions: Read the following excerpt from the Civil Rights Address given by President John F. Kennedy. Then answer questions 33 through 37.

The heart of the question is whether all Americans are to be afforded equal rights and equal opportunities, whether we are going to treat our fellow Americans as we want to be treated. If an American, because his skin is dark, cannot eat lunch in a restaurant open to the public, if he cannot send his children to the best public school available, if he cannot vote for the public officials who will represent him, if, in short, he cannot enjoy the full and free life which all of us want, then who among us would be content to have the color of his skin changed and stand in his place? Who among us would then be content with the counsels of patience and delay?

One hundred years of delay have passed since President Lincoln freed the slaves, yet their heirs, their grandsons, are not fully free. They are not yet freed from the bonds of injustice. They are not yet freed from social and economic oppression. And this Nation, for all its hopes and all its boasts, will not be fully free until all its citizens are free.

We preach freedom around the world, and we mean it, and we cherish our freedom here at home, but are we to say to the world, and much more importantly, to each other that this is the land of the free except for the Negroes; that we have no second-class citizens except Negroes[1]; that we have no class or caste system, no ghettoes, no master race except with respect to Negroes?

Now the time has come for this Nation to fulfill its promise. The events in Birmingham and elsewhere have so increased the cries for equality that no city or State or legislative body can prudently choose to ignore them. The fires of frustration and discord are burning in every city, North and South, where legal remedies are not at hand. Redress is sought in the streets, in demonstrations, parades, and protests which create tensions and threaten violence and threaten lives.

We face, therefore, a moral crisis as a country and a people. It cannot be met by repressive police action. It cannot be left to increased demonstrations in the streets. It cannot be quieted by token moves or talk. It is a time to act in the Congress, in your

State and local legislative body and, above all, in all of our daily lives. It is not enough to pin the blame on others, to say this is a problem of one section of the country or another, or deplore the facts that we face. A great change is at hand, and our task, our obligation, is to make that revolution, that change, peaceful and constructive for all. Those who do nothing are inviting shame, as well as violence. Those who act boldly are recognizing right, as well as reality.

---

[1]President Kennedy delivered this speech in June of 1963, an era when African Americans were referred to as "Negroes," the outdated term used in this passage.

33. The purpose of this address is to

A. compare

B. inform

C. persuade

D. entertain

34. Another name for an *address* as used in the directions of this passage is

A. a letter

B. an e-mail

C. a memo

D. a speech

35. Read the following sentence:

One hundred years of delay have passed since President Lincoln freed the slaves, yet their heirs, their grandsons, are not fully free.

The word *delay* in this sentence means the same as

A. waiting

B. continuing

C. decline

D. improvement

36. The main idea of this address is that
   A. everyone in America deserves to be treated equally
   B. President Lincoln did much to advance African Americans
   C. all American citizens have the same freedoms
   D. people are still prejudiced in parts of America

37. Read the following phrase:

   The fires of frustration and discord are burning in every city

   This is an example of a
   A. hyperbole
   B. metaphor
   C. simile
   D. rhyme

Directions: Read the following excerpt from Edna Ferber's interview with Harry Houdini, the famous escape artist. Then answer questions 38 through 41.

Houdini, who left this noon for New York, arrived in Appleton, his birthplace, Wednesday afternoon, accompanied by his brother Theodore, who travels with him and assists him in his performances. He spent the time here looking up old friends and renewing old associations. In August he will sail for Europe where he has a two-year contract and will give no performances while in America. He is resting here and one can see how he needs a period of quiet when one talks to him, for he is a quick, nervous chap, inclined to jump when an unexpected noise is heard and to shut his eyes until they are almost closed....

"My first performance? Well I remember it well as if it had taken place yesterday. I am earning now, from $900 to $2000 a week, but my first performance brought me slightly less than that. It took place in an old field across the track in the Sixth Ward and I did a contortionist act, giving three performances, for which Jack Hoeffler, who was managing them, as now, paid me exactly 35 cents." Houdini threw back his head and chuckled reminiscently and thought of the $2000 per.

"What was your most difficult feat, the most difficult escape you ever made?" was asked.

"I think my escape from the Siberian Transport was my most difficult performance. I was placed in the great vault usually assigned to political prisoners, and when the great door was shut, I had the hardest time of my life, perhaps, in releasing myself. But nevertheless, it took me 18 minutes to walk out, and face the dazed officials.

"I think that in a year I may retire. I cannot take my money with me when I die and I wish to enjoy it, with my family, while I live. I should prefer living in Germany to any other country, though I am an American, and am loyal to my country. I like the German people and customs. Why don't I go then? Why, it is too far away from my mother, who lives in New York City with a couple of my young brothers."

And right there you have the whole charm of Ehrich Weiss. It is worth all the sermons in the world to hear him speak of his mother. All his plans, all his successes, he weaves about that mother of his. The fortune he has made within the past ten years, he does not speak of as benefiting himself, "My mother can have everything that she wants," he says. Of his father, Rabbi Weiss, who died, he speaks just as affectionately and reverently, and in these days of rush and hurry and often disrespect for old age, it is pleasant to hear such filial words.

38. Why was Houdini visiting Appleton?

    A. he was giving his first performance

    B. he accompanied his brother

    C. he was relaxing and visiting friends

    D. he was taking care of his mother

39. What can be inferred from Houdini's laugh after he explains how much money he made for his first performance?

    A. he realizes how his pay has improved

    B. he realizes that he is more popular now

    C. he realizes how his life has changed

    D. all of the above

40. Houdini doesn't move to Germany because

    A. he loves America more than anywhere else

    B. he hasn't made enough money

    C. he does not want to be separated from his family

    D. he is very loyal to his country

41. Read the following sentence:

    Of his father, Rabbi Weiss, who died, he speaks just as affectionately and reverently, and in these days of rush and hurry and often disrespect for old age, it is pleasant to hear such filial words.

    Based on the context clues, the word filial most likely means

    A. impolite

    B. devoted

    C. urgent

    D. humble

BOOK 2: LISTENING AND WRITING MECHANICS

> *Note to Reader:* Remove the directions and story from the rest of the test, leaving the note pages for the student to take notes on while you read the directions and passage twice.

8 Multiple-Choice Questions

3 Short-Response Questions

30 Minutes to Complete—Work Until You Come to Book 3.

Directions: **You will hear a passage called "Mohandas K. Gandhi" by Sarah Krajewski. You will listen to the passage two times. You may take notes at any time as you listen to the passage. Then you will use your notes to help you answer the questions that follow. Your answers to these questions will show your understanding of the passage.**

Here is a word you will need to know as you listen to the passage:

▪ **partition—separation or division**

The correct answers, with explanations, follow this test on pages 227–229.

MOHANDAS K. GANDHI

Sarah Krajewski

One day in April of 1930, Mohandas Karamchand Gandhi knelt down by the Arabian Sea and picked up salt that had been left by the ocean. By doing that, Gandhi broke a law that prohibited Indians from getting salt anywhere except from the British. Gandhi's act of picking up salt symbolized his role as a peaceful protester to injustice everywhere. Nonviolent actions like this earned him the new name Mahatma, or "great soul."

Born on October 2, 1869, Gandhi was the youngest child in his Hindu family. When he was thirteen, his parents arranged for him to marry a twelve-year-old named Kasturba. Though they married young, they did not have their first child until 1888. Right after the birth of their first child, Gandhi left for London and began taking law classes at the University of London. Once there, Gandhi became a vegetarian, and he studied vegetarianism to justify his diet. Throughout his studies he read Buddhist and Hindu scriptures, some of which became his moral guidebook later on.

After he completed his schooling, Gandhi returned to India and began working for an Indian firm in the colony of Natal in South Africa. Getting involved in politics began to change his thinking, so he decided to stay in South Africa. At this point the legislature was writing a bill that would deny voting rights to Indians. Gandhi failed to stop this, but he did draw attention to the inequality Indians had to deal with. He created the Natal Indian Congress in 1894 to help fight for the rights of Indians. Soon afterward, Gandhi went back to India to bring his wife and children back to Africa.

When World War I began, Gandhi returned to India to start a new phase in his life. At first he supported the British and their use of Indians in the British army, but when the government began to imprison Indians without trial, Gandhi called for a *satyagraha*, or peaceful protest. The government responded violently, though, and the deaths shocked Gandhi. This forced him to stop his protest, but he succeeded in teaching Indians to stand up for themselves.

Gandhi's fight for equal rights continued, but he did not play a major role in the fight for independence until 1929, when he launched a new nonviolent protest against the tax on salt. Gandhi's famous push against the salt tax included a 250-mile march to a seaside village, where he made his own salt. Many Indians participated in this march; 60,000 people were put in jail for marching with Gandhi. Afterward, the government created the Gandhi-Irwin Pact of 1931, which allowed all political prisoners to be freed if they stopped protesting.

By the 1930s, Gandhi found more peaceful ways to get his point across. In 1933 he decided to fast for 21 days to protest the Indian government's treatment of Indians. This fast by Gandhi was the first of many. Because of his protests, in 1934 the British tried to take Gandhi's life on three separate occasions.

In 1934 Jawaharlal Nehru became the new leader of the Indian National Congress. Gandhi disagreed with many of Nehru's ideas but still thought he was better than other possible leaders of the movement. By this point Gandhi threw himself into educating rural parts of India. He lived very modestly in Sevagram, a small village in central India, for five years.

Even though Gandhi was a Hindu, he kept friendships within both the Hindu and Muslim communities. He was opposed to any form of partition, but unfortunately the Indian National Congress agreed to a partition agreement in 1947 that divided British India into two separate states: India and Pakistan. Gandhi also saw the importance in each and every tradition. He once said that he was not just a Hindu but also a Christian, Muslim, and Jew. Gandhi was more spiritual than religious, though, and saw the search for peace in every facet of life. Many consider him the father of modern India. Alas, this preacher of nonviolence met a violent end. On January 30, 1948, Gandhi was shot and killed by a fanatic while walking to his evening prayers.

Not many countries were freed from colonial power by nonviolent measures, but India was; this was due to the vast power and stature of the humble Mahatma Gandhi. He inspired a generation to use nonviolence to achieve positive change, and he had a great impact on other inspirational leaders, such as Martin Luther King Jr. of the American civil rights movement.

NOTES

NOTES

1. Although Gandhi studied many religions, the religion he was born into was

   A. Christian

   B. Hindu

   C. Muslim

   D. Jewish

2. Read the following sentence:

   At first he supported the British and their use of Indians in the British army, but when the government began to imprison Indians without trial, Gandhi called for a *satyagraha*, or peaceful protest.

   Based on this sentence, one can infer that the country of India was being governed by

   A. protesters

   B. India

   C. Indians

   D. Great Britain

3. The following words could be used to describe Mahatma Gandhi except

   A. aggressive

   B. nonviolent

   C. peaceful

   D. inspirational

4. Many consider Gandhi the father of modern India because he

   A. had an impact on other leaders like Martin Luther King Jr.

   B. helped free India from the colonial control of Great Britain

   C. showed the Indian people how to protest peacefully

   D. staged a nonviolent protest against the salt tax

5. Read the following sentence:

> Nonviolent actions like this earned him the new name Mahatma, or "great soul."

Why is the phrase *great soul* in quotes?

A. It is part of a dialogue.

B. It is a title.

C. It is a proper noun.

D. It is a definition.

6. Which sentence has proper capitalization?

A. Ghandi left for London and began taking law classes at the University of London.

B. Ghandi left for London and began taking Law classes at the University of London.

C. Ghandi left for London and began taking Law Classes at the University Of London.

D. Ghandi left for London and began taking law classes at the university of London.

7. Read the following sentence:

> When World War I began, Gandhi returned to London to start a new phase in his life.

There is a comma separating *When World War I began* from the rest of the sentence because it is

A. a compound sentence

B. a complex sentence

C. a dependent clause

D. an independent clause

8. Which sentence uses the correct homonym?

   A. Though they married young, they did not have there first child until 1888.

   B. Though they married young, they didn't have there first child until 1888.

   C. Though they married young, they did not have they're first child until 1888.

   D. Though they married young, they did not have their first child until 1888.

9. In the chart below, list three things that Mohandas Gandhi did to fight for equal rights for Indians.

Mohandas Gandhi's Actions

10. Mohandas K. Gandhi earned the name Mahatma, or "great soul," because of his nonviolent protests against injustice. Based on his actions, why was this name fitting for him? Use details from the passage to support your answer.

_____

_____

_____

_____

_____

_____

11. The last sentence of the passage states

    Gandhi has a great impact on other inspirational leaders, such as Martin Luther King Jr. of the American Civil Rights Movement.

    What character trait did Gandhi display that made him an inspiration to other leaders like Martin Luther King Jr.? Use details from the passage to support your answer.

    _____

    _____

    _____

    _____

    _____

    _____

    _____

    _____

BOOK 3: READING AND WRITING

4 Short-Response Questions

1 Extended-Response Question

60 Minutes to Complete—Work to the End of the Test.

Directions: Book 3 asks you to write about two passages you will read. When you write your responses, be sure to

■ Clearly organize your ideas

■ Clearly express your ideas

■ Completely and accurately answer the questions

■ Support the ideas in your responses by examples from the passage or passages and, if required by question, your experiences and opinions

■ Make your writing enjoyable and interesting to the reader

One passage you will read is a poem by Ella Wheeler Wilcox called "A Baby in the House." In this poem, the narrator describes the house and actions of a mother and father. The other passage is an interview with a mother of a child with autism. Use what you learn from the passages to answer questions 1 through 5.

A BABY IN THE HOUSE

Ella Wheeler Wilcox

I knew that a baby was hid in the house;
Though I saw no cradle and heard no cry,
But the husband went tiptoeing round like a mouse,
And the good wife was humming a soft lullaby;
And there was a look on the face of that mother
That I knew could mean only *one* thing, and no other.

"The *mother*," I said to myself; for I knew
That the woman before me was certainly that,
For there lay in the corner a tiny cloth shoe,
And I saw on the stand such a wee little hat;
And the beard of the husband said plain as could be,
"Two fat, chubby hands have been tugging at me."

And he took from his pocket a gay picture-book,
And a dog that would bark if you pulled on a string;
And the wife laid them up with such a pleased look;
And I said to myself, "There is no other thing
But a babe that could bring about all this, and so
That one is in hiding here somewhere, I know."

I stayed but a moment, and saw nothing more,
And heard not a sound, yet I knew I was right;
What else could the shoe mean that lay on the floor,
The book and the toy, and the faces so bright?
And what made the husband as still as a mouse?
I am sure, *very* sure, there's a babe in that house.

1. In the chart that follows, identify one tangible (something concrete that you can touch) and one intangible (something that is apparent but you cannot touch) piece of evidence from the poem that there was a baby in the house.

Tangible Evidence	Intangible Evidence

2. The reader is never told exactly who the narrator of the poem is. Using clues from the poem, who might the narrator in the poem be? Describe the evidence that supports your response.

_____

_____

_____

_____

_____

_____

_____

Autism is a developmental disorder that keeps children from developing the same way other children do. Children with autism usually have difficulty communicating verbally and nonverbally and do not interact socially with others in typical ways. They require special care, love, and education.

AN INTERVIEW WITH A PARENT OF A CHILD WITH AUTISM

Cindy Lassonde

Interviewer: Hello, Mrs. Reynolds. Hi, Casey.

Mrs. Reynolds: Hello. Casey says, "Hello. How are you?"

Interviewer: Mrs. Reynolds, can you tell us about your daughter and yourself?

Mrs. Reynolds: Hi. This is my daughter Casey, and I am Cindy Reynolds. Casey is seven years old and has been diagnosed with autism. Casey is in a class with other children with developmental delays in our local school district. Academically, she is a very smart little girl. Aren't you, sweetie? She does work that is above her grade level. But, she has some severe sensory issues that we take very good care to avoid. Don't we, Casey?

Interviewer: Can you tell us a little about these issues?

Mrs. Reynolds: She likes to watch things and has to be constantly stimulated. Like television. She watches the movements and colors on television. She goes to sleep with a television playing in her room; she cannot fall asleep in silence. She doesn't like things to touch her very much. She doesn't tolerate, for example, certain kinds of fabrics next to her skin. Casey likes light cotton clothes only. When she touches any other kind of material, she gets very irritated at us. But that's okay, isn't it Casey? We figure things out as we go. When Casey doesn't like something, what do we do, Casey? We put it outside. That's what we tell her. We say, "It's all gone. Daddy put it outside." That seems to soothe her when she gets upset.

Interviewer: Can you tell us about Casey's friends?

Mrs. Reynolds: The girl is asking about your friends, Casey. Let's tell her about your friends. Okay? There are lots of kids at school. Aren't there, Casey? When it's playtime at school, Casey plays next to the other children. The teachers call this parallel play. She likes to be near other children but she will kind of do her own thing instead of interacting with them. That's her special way of playing. Like when you go outside at recess time, Casey, you like to do what the other children are doing. Right? So, you sit next to them.

Interviewer: What has been your greatest moment with Casey?

Mrs. Reynolds: My greatest moment was when she was born. My husband and I are so grateful to have Casey in our lives. We just love her so much. We don't know what we would do without her. She can be a challenge some times, but what kid isn't? Right, Casey?

3. What do we learn about children with autism from the interview? What do we still not know? Complete the following chart with one characteristic we know and one we do not know based on the passage.

What We Know about Autism	What We Do Not Know about Autism

4. Casey does not speak during the interview. How does Mrs. Reynolds try to make her part of the interview?

_____

_____

_____

_____

_____

_____

_____

PLANNING PAGE

You may PLAN your writing for question 5 on this page. Write your final response on the lines on the next pages.

5. Parenting can be very rewarding and yet very difficult. "A Baby in the House" and the interview with Casey's mother in "An Interview with a Parent of a Child with Autism" both provided windows into what it might be like to be a parent. Write an essay comparing and contrasting the two passages and how they each represent parenthood.

In your answer, be sure to

■ describe how the family in "A Baby in the House" represented what it is like to be parents;

■ describe how Casey's mother represented what it is like to be a parent;

■ compare the two passages by telling how they are similar;

■ contrast the two passages by telling how they are different;

■ use evidence from both passages to support your response;

■ check your grammar, spelling, and punctuation.

_____

_____

_____

_____

_____

_____

_____

_____

_____

_____

_____

_____

_____

_____

_____

_____

_____

_____

_____

_____

_____

_____

_____

_____

_____

_____

_____

_____

_____

_____

_____

_____

_____

ANSWERS AND EXPLANATIONS

BOOK 1: READING

"Arithmetic"

1. **A** The phrases "squeeze from" and "until you get the answer" imply the student is struggling. Writing a list of numbers doesn't involve getting an answer. There is no reference to a blackboard or calculator being used.

2. **D** The phrase "hope you don't lose it" implies that arithmetic can be stressful for the author.

3. **A** Choice A is the only answer that used the word *like* to compare unlike things.

4. **B** The repetition of "No no no," "nix, nix, nix," and so on, shows frustration. There is no evidence that the author is either relaxed, melancholy, or nostalgic.

Excerpt from *Lou Paduano's Short Story*

5. **B** Choice A implies a light, vacation tone, whereas the excerpt is mysterious and dangerous in tone. Although Betsy's sacrifices (choice C) are mentioned, they don't constitute enough of the story to make that the title. There is no evidence that nuclear science is involved (choice D); plus, "Nuclear Science" is a title more for an expository essay than for this type of narrative story. Choice B reflects the whole passage because it leads up to the dreaded explosion. Also, it might be used to reflect Horace's smile at the end. Did Betsy dread seeing his smile?

6. **A** The passage states, "it could only end this way," suggesting that the couple will die from the explosion. The characters do not appear scared; Horace and Betsy continue to sit there as Betsy observes Horace's smile. Finally, there are no clues that Horace and Betsy will jump off the cliff for any reason.

7. **A** The author doesn't give readers a direct explanation of the reason Horace smiled at the end. Either choice B or C could be how Horace feels, but the author lets the reader interpret Horace's reaction to the explosion. Choice D is incorrect because the author doesn't give the reader any indication that Betsy might smile also or feel the same way Horace does.

"The Thief and the Innkeeper"

8. **C** "Pray wait . . ." indicates that the thief is pleading rather than grabbing, insulting, or demanding.

9. **B** Although the thief was planning to rob the innkeeper of his coat, the innkeeper didn't know this. Therefore, choice A is not correct. Readers know the innkeeper was afraid he was going to get attacked because the passage says he "became greatly alarmed and, rising from his seat, attempted to run away." The author gives us no clues that the innkeeper was afraid because the thief gave him his clothes or that the thief was insane.

10. **A** The innkeeper shouldn't have believed the thief's tale. Not every tale should be taken to heart (choice A). Choices B, C, and D are not correct because there are no supporting details to affirm these morals in this fable.

11. **D** If the wolf, innkeeper, or thief were telling this story, it would be written in first-person narrative, using "I" to replace the character weaving the fable.

12. **A** The innkeeper is friendly (choice A) because he takes the time to talk to the thief. They have a conversation before the thief tries to trick the innkeeper. We cannot assume he is ignorant or selfish because the author doesn't say anything to indicate that. We never hear the innkeeper become angry. Instead, he runs away at the end.

13. **D** Over time, the conversation begins to droop. The author tells us the thief yawns, showing the innkeeper he is losing interest.

14. **B** Phrases like "left his new coat in the thief's hand and ran as fast as he could" and "the thief made off with the coat" indicate that the thief wasn't being polite or helping the innkeeper off with his coat.

Excerpt from *Black Beauty, Young Folks' Edition*

15. **A** Black Beauty is telling the story in first-person narrative.

16. **C** Although choices A, B, and D are mentioned, overall the passage is about Black Beauty's early home. The passage includes his mother's advice, the six colts, and the master as details about his early home.

17. **B** Black Beauty isn't yet being trained; he is too young (choice A). His days are rather carefree, without hardships (choice C). He has no new freedoms that he didn't have before (choice D).

18. **B** Choice A says he's never forgotten her advice, but that doesn't show how he feels about her. If she'd given bad advice, he could still say he's never forgotten it. Choices C and D are just statements of fact. They give no evidence of feelings. Choice B says he knew she was wise, which indicates he respects her for that.

19. **C** The description of the pleasant meadow, sleeping near his mother, and playing with his friends indicates things were peaceful. There are no clues to indicate that choices A, B, or D are true.

20. **A** She tells him ". . . I hope you will grow up gentle and good. Never learn bad ways. Do your work with a good will. Lift your feet up well when you trot, and never bite or kick even in play."

"President Barack Obama: An Emerging Leader"

21. **C** Choice A cannot be correct because Obama was already nominated and elected. Choice B is not correct because there is no persuasive voice in the passage; it is strictly informational. Choice D points to only a small part of the passage about Obama's work in Chicago. Choice C is correct because this passage is largely informational.

22. **B** Telling about Obama's childhood can only serve the purpose of demonstrating how his background may influence his goals and views. Choices A, C, and D are unsupported.

23. **D** The passage says, ". . . Barack Obama decided that law was a medium that could facilitate activism and community organization."

24. **C** Although choices A, B, and D are from the passage, choice C provides the broadest support of the main idea.

25. **A** Declaring candidacy means announcing that one is running for office. Context clues in the passage support this meaning.

26. **B** Although choices A, C, and D are included in the passage, most of the information is about Obama. Therefore, a person writing a paper about Obama would get the most information from this passage.

27. **C** Understanding his own multiracial and multicultural background will help him understand and relate to the diversities in America.

28. **A** As a community organizer, he helped those from poor neighborhoods receive the services they were entitled to from the government.

"My Castle"

29. **A** The reader can infer that it is a group of clouds because the narrator describes lying on his back and looking up into the blue sky to see his castle.

30. **D** The castle lifts the narrator's spirits because he states that when his heart "is heavy with care," or unhappy, he "dwells," or thinks of, his castle in the air.

31. **C** The castle is most important to him, so it does not matter what others think.

32. **B** The mood is contented, because the narrator knows the castle in the sky makes him happy, and he is not concerned with what others think or believe.

Excerpt from Kennedy's Address

33. **C** The questioning and reasoning tone of the address is meant to persuade and motivate others to action.

34. **D** Speech is the correct answer, because audience is the country. The president would not send a memo, e-mail, or letter to everyone in the country. He would, however, make a speech.

35. **A** *Waiting* is a synonym for *delay*.

36. **A** The concept that everyone in America should receive equal rights is mentioned in various ways throughout the address.

37. **B** A metaphor is a direct comparison between two things. In this case, the emotions of frustration and discord are being compared to fire because of their strength.

Excerpt from An Interview with Houdini

38. **C** The first paragraph states that he was resting and "looking up old friends" while in Appleton.

39. **D** Although the reader could assume that Houdini is laughing over his change in salary, any of the answers could be possible inferences.

40. **C** Houdini states that his mother and a couple of his young brothers live in New York City, and Germany is too far away from them.

41. **B** *Devoted* is the best choice. *Filial* relates to a son or daughter, and *devoted* means to show tremendous love and care for someone or something. This is how Houdini's words are described when he, as a son, refers to his late father.

BOOK 2: LISTENING AND WRITING MECHANICS

"Mohandas K. Gandhi"

1. **B** The beginning of the listening passage states that Gandhi was born into a Hindu family.

2. **D** The sentences mention the British use of Indians in the British army. The British government is also mentioned. Therefore, the answer is Great Britain.

3. **A** The word *aggressive* is the opposite of *nonviolent*, which is used several times in the passage to describe Gandhi. He is also referred to as *peaceful* and *inspirational*.

4. **B** Although Gandhi did all of the other things mentioned, the reason he is referred to as the father of modern India is because all of his protests were aimed at gaining equal rights for Indians and ended the mistreatment Indians received under British control.

5. **D** The phrase is in quotes because it is the literal meaning of the name *Mahatma*.

6. **A** The first sentence has proper capitalization. *Ghandi, London,* and the *University of London* are all proper nouns that need to be capitalized.

7. **C** *When World War I began* is a dependent clause. Because it begins with the word *when*, the phrase cannot stand alone as a sentence and therefore is not an independent clause, nor is it a part of a compound sentence or a complex sentence.

8. **D** The correct homonym from the *there, their, they're* series is *their*. The word is used to show possession in the sentence, so it needs the possessive pronoun *their*. *There* shows location, and *they're* is a contraction meaning *they are*.

9. These are some of the things that could be included in the graphic organizer that lists what Gandhi did for equal rights for Indians:

Mohandas Gandhi's Actions
Created the Natal Indian Congress in 1894 to fight for the voting rights of Indians
Called for a satyagraha, or peaceful protest, when the British government imprisoned Indians without trial
Staged a 250-mile march to protest the tax on salt
Fasted for 21 days to protest the Indian government's treatment of Indians
Threw himself into educating rural parts of India

10. The short response to this question should be similar to the following:

Mohandas K. Gandhi earned the name Mahatma, or "great soul," because of his nonviolent protests against injustice. This name is fitting for him because he did everything in his power to stop the unequal treatment of the Indians by the British and Indian governments. First, he created the Natal Indian Congress in 1894 to fight for the voting rights of Indians. Later, he used satyagraha, or peaceful protest, when the British government imprisoned Indians without trial. Gandhi also led marches and fasted in order to win equal rights for Indians. None of these protests used violence to make a point. Therefore, the name Mahatma, or Great Soul, is appropriate to describe Gandhi.

11. The short response to this question should be similar to the following:

> One of the character traits that made Gandhi an inspiration to other leaders was his persistence. He did not give up even when his fight for equal rights for Indians was physically difficult for him. For example, when he protested the salt tax, he walked an exhausting 250 miles. When he wanted to protest the government's treatment of Indians, he fasted for 21 days. These peaceful protests were difficult on his body, but his mind stayed strong and he was determined to fight for what he believed in. Other leaders saw Gandhi's inner strength and tried to behave as he did to achieve their goals.

Other character traits that could be used in the answer include determination, bravery, and tolerance.

BOOK 3: READING AND WRITING

"A Baby in the House"

1. The graphic organizer should be completed with details directly from the passage. Here are some of the possible answers. Only one response is required in each column, though.

Tangible Evidence	Intangible Evidence
There was a tiny cloth shoe in the corner.	The husband tiptoed around the house.
There was a wee little hat on the stand.	The wife hummed a lullaby.
The husband had a picture book and dog toy.	The wife's face had a look like no other.
	The husband's beard looked like it had been pulled on.
	The wife looked pleased at the husband when he took out the book and toy.

2. The short response to this question should be similar to the following:

Although readers are never told exactly who the narrator is, from the poem we can tell it is someone who does not know the family well. Otherwise, the person would already know if there were a baby. Also, the narrator wasn't in the house long enough to hear the baby cry or see the baby in person. The baby must have been in another room sleeping. The narrator may have been a door-to-door salesperson or a delivery person who was visiting the house briefly. Finally, because the narrator never seems to find out if there is a baby or not for sure, it seems he or she was someone who would probably not be invited to return to the house as a friend or close acquaintance might be.

"An Interview with a Parent of a Child with Autism"

3. The graphic organizer should be completed with details directly from the passage. Here are some of the possible answers. Only one response is required for each column, though.

What We Know About Autism	What We Do Not Know About Autism
Children with autism have trouble interacting with other children. They participate in parallel play around other children. Children with autism can be very smart in school.	We do not know how children become autistic. We do not know why autism affects a child's senses.

4. The short response to this question should be similar to the following:

Mrs. Reynolds keeps trying to pull Casey into the interview by asking her questions. She keeps saying, "Right, Casey?" to confirm with Casey that she is answering correctly. Mrs. Reynolds also phrases things in a very positive way so it doesn't sound like she's talking badly about Casey in front of her but instead is answering for Casey. She speaks directly for Casey also when she says, "Hello. How are you?" to the interviewer. These behaviors all show that Mrs. Reynolds is trying to make Casey part of the interview.

5. The extended response should be similar to the following:

The two passages show that parenting can be very rewarding and yet very difficult. "A Baby in the House" and the interview with Casey's mother in "An Interview with a Parent of a Child with Autism" illustrate several views of parenthood.

The family in "A Baby in the House" represents what it is like to be parents. The narrator of the poem describes the types of articles you would find around a house when there is a baby in the house, such as toys and small articles of clothing. It also describes how people act when a baby is around, particularly when the baby is sleeping. The father tiptoed around and the mother hummed lullabies.

In "An Interview with a Parent of a Child with Autism," Casey's mother describes what it is like to love and take care of a child who has some developmental delays. She explains how she provides for Casey's physical and emotional needs. She provides cotton clothes that Casey can tolerate, and she calms Casey by saying, "Daddy put it outside."

When the two passages are compared, you can see how both the parents in the poem and Casey's parents have deep love for their children. Parents show their love by the things they do for them. The baby's parents must play with the baby with the dog toy and read to him or her from the picture book. Mrs. Reynolds tried to include Casey in the interview by asking her questions and answering for her when she couldn't answer herself.

When the two passages are contrasted, you can see how parenting must be different for both families. There is no talk or sign of the difficulties the parents in the poem experience, although we know babies can be trying also. Because of the questions the interviewer asks Mrs. Reynolds, however, we hear Mrs. Reynolds explain some issues she has to take care of with Casey. For example, she has to calm Casey when she gets irritated and she has to constantly keep her busy. We know this when she talks about having the television set on.

Parenting can be rewarding, but it can also be difficult. These two passages illustrate both views of parenthood.

INDEX